"A timely read for th a season when we are daily seeing the enemy in full attack, Karen does a beautiful job of reminding us He is with us in every trial. Karen fills each chapter with scripture and personal stories, and beautifully points the reader to Jesus. Karen writes from her heart and the truth that comes from Jesus Christ. An excellent read for anyone no matter where they are in their walk with Christ."

—**Cheryl Goss,**
Founder and President of Connecting Ministries,
www.connectingministries.org

"I laughed out loud and quietly cried as I walked through these pages filled with God's hope and faithfulness over so many trials of life. Karen gives us a front row seat to God's redemptive story. Escape into a powerful, lifelong journey of two people who simply kept saying yes to Jesus. As I finish Karen's book, I am left with a sober reminder that God will continue to challenge us through our own life's circumstances. Grab this book, find your warm place in the sun, and brace to experience God's redemptive story in your own life."

—**Charny Beck,** MSSW, LCSW-S,
Licensed Clinical Social Worker, pastor's wife

"This book is a real look at real life. Life can be messy, but Karen Oak reminds us that God shows up in the ordinary and has a plan to guide us through the most challenging of circumstances. This book will help you deposit God's biblical truth right into the center of life's most challenging moments."

—**Doug Page,**
Senior Pastor,
First Baptist Church, Grapevine, Texas

"Honest . . . real . . . compelling. Karen's journey through the valleys and high places will help you understand your own. You owe it to yourself and those you love to dig in, take notes, and grow exponentially."

—**Dr. Roger Patterson,**
Senior Pastor, West University Baptist & Crosspoint Church,
Author of *A Minute of Vision for Men*

A *warm place* IN THE SUN

FINDING JOY *in the* STRUGGLES

KAREN OAK

LUCIDBOOKS

A Warm Place in the Sun
Finding Joy in the Struggles

Copyright © 2020 by Karen Oak

Published by Lucid Books in Houston, TX
www.LucidBooksPublishing.com

ISBN: 978-1-63296-423-6
eISBN: 978-1-63296-424-3

Unless otherwise noted, all Scripture quotations are taken from the ESV Bible®, (The Holy Bible, English Standard Version®), Copyright © 2001 by Crossway, a publishing ministry of Good News Publishers. Used by permission. All rights reserved.

Scripture quotations marked (CSB) are taken from the Christian Standard Bible®, Copyright © 2017 by Holman Bible Publishers. Used by permission. Christian Standard Bible® and CSB® are federally registered trademarks of Holman Bible Publishers.

Scripture quotations marked (NIV) are taken from the Holy Bible, New International Version®, NIV®. Copyright ©1973, 1978, 1984, 2011 by Biblica, Inc.™ Used by permission of Zondervan. All rights reserved worldwide. www.zondervan.com The "NIV" and "New International Version" are trademarks registered in the United States Patent and Trademark Office by Biblica, Inc.™

Special Sales: Most Lucid Books titles are available in special quantity discounts. Custom imprinting or excerpting can also be done to fit special needs. For standard bulk orders, go to www.lucidbooksbulk.com. For specialty press or large orders, contact Lucid Books at books@lucidbookspublishing.com.

To Chuck
My husband, my travel partner on this journey of life,
my encourager, my best friend, my one true love

Table of Contents

Special Thanks

My first thanks and praise are to my Lord and Savior, Jesus Christ. I thank him for my call to salvation and the secure and abundant life he brings. I also thank him for the call to write this book and for sustaining me and guiding me through the journey.

I am overwhelmed with gratitude to my family— my husband, Chuck; our daughters, Bonnie and Kelley; their husbands, Frank and DJ; and my mom, Betty Cole. Thank you for allowing me to transparently share so much of our lives. Each of you is such a blessing to me.

Thank you, Dr. Roger Patterson for being my amazing pastor, cheerleader, advisor, and friend. You kept me going with your prayers, direction, and encouraging words.

I must include my "Tribe"—Linda Rodekohr, Margaret Robinson, Dana Walker, Kim McAuliffe, Robin Phillips, Kathryn James, Susie Edworthy, and

Nancy Ainslie. Thank you for the prayers, edits, and encouragement throughout this process.

Special thanks to Mike and Eva Quearry for the generous offering of your beach condo for my writing getaways. What a blessing it was to me!

Thank you, Justin Kellough for the beautiful "one sheet" you designed that helped get me on my way.

Finally, thank you Lucid Books for partnering with me to make this book a reality.

I am blessed!

Introduction

I had a dog, a Shih Tzu named Hershey, or, according to his papers, Herschel Kiss. He was a precious, cuddly, reddish-brown puppy that loved to lick everyone and everything. It didn't take much imagination to give him a name, especially for a girl who loves chocolate. He was an adorable little lap dog that also loved to run around the house chasing his little stuffed bear when we tossed it. Once he had it in his mouth, rather than bring it back, he growled as only a cute little dog can and shook it back and forth so hard and fast that it slapped him on either side of his head. He loved to nestle into the clean laundry on the sofa for rest time, but when he heard the kibble falling into his dish, he ran the length of the sofa, took a flying leap off the end, and skidded across the wood floor as he scrambled at full speed into the kitchen. He was a fun, spirited, happy little dog.

At the young age of four, Hershey's retinas spontaneously detached, leaving him in total darkness. He had an expectedly rough time adjusting to his new world of black. He was continually bumping into walls and furniture and afraid to venture outside without someone by his side. Our little spunky dog was traumatized. Gradually and over time, he learned, largely from memory, how to navigate his world without sight. He became so proficient in his new reality that guests in our home didn't even realize Hershey couldn't see. He knew where his crate and food dish were in the kitchen, and he agilely jumped up on the sofa to curl up in his favorite spot—the pile of clean laundry. He easily found his way to the door to go outside, and he even found his way around the backyard unassisted. His blindness gradually became normal to all of us, and we began to take his newfound abilities for granted.

There was one achievement, however, that never failed to amaze me. On any given sunny day, I could walk into the living room and find Hershey lying on the floor right where the sun was shining down through the window. Keep in mind that the sunshine moved throughout the day according to the angle of the sun in relationship to the large-paned window. That didn't matter. Hershey always found it. How did he do that? He couldn't see. He couldn't even discern light. Yet in the midst of his darkness, Hershey was always able to find that warm place in the sun.

How like us, I thought. As we pass through the most difficult, darkest times of our lives, God will provide us with that warm place in the sun. As we struggle to navigate through the black ugliness of our days, he will be that place for us where we feel his comfort, his peace, and his strength warming our inner being.

God promised to be our light in the darkness. He promised us Jesus, who would become the Light of the world. "The people who walked in darkness have seen a great light; those who dwelt in a land of deep darkness, on them has light shone" (Isa. 9:2).

Are you walking in darkness? "Where's my warm place in the sun?" you may be thinking. Your circumstances may be dark, painful, and seemingly without hope. How do you find that warm, comforting place where God encourages and gives strength? It begins with a simple acknowledgment that he is God—that he is here loving you and looking out for you, even when you can't see him.

Hershey would have never found that place in the sun if he hadn't searched for it. From his past experience, before his blind darkness, he knew the sunshine was there. He had experienced its warm comfort and rested there many times before. He just had to find it.

Do you know Jesus? Have you experienced the purpose, joy, and comfort that he brings? Then you know, as his Word promises, that he will never leave you. Perhaps you don't know him personally. Perhaps you only know about him. If that is the case, let me introduce you to my best friend. He is the source of my joy and comfort. Without him, this book and these words would have no meaning. More importantly, without him, I would not have survived the struggles, trials, and dark, ugly days of my life, nor would I have experienced the extreme joy and happiness of the good times and the many blessings he has bestowed.

First, you must understand how much the God of all creation loves you. Before the world began, he had a plan to create a realm of time and space in which he could fellowship and pour out his love on humankind. He created this earth with you and me in mind. Think of the effort you put in to create a space called your home, where you and your family feel comfort, pleasure, and love. You choose the color scheme that soothes and the sofa that cuddles you when you sit. You choose the throw pillow that brings a smile to your face and the carpeting that hugs your toes. That's what God had in mind for us when he created earth—our home. He crafted the mountains and the seas for us. He designed each herb and flower, each fish and puppy dog with you in mind.

He intricately designed a man, creating him from dust, and then a woman to live in partnership with the man. These people were to be the beneficiaries of all God's loving creation. They were to be his children with whom he could commune and who would bring him joy.

Sadly, sin broke this sweet fellowship with a perfect God. Every human has at some point lived, walked, or acted in disobedience to our holy God. "For all have sinned and fall short of the glory of God" (Rom. 3:23). Sin and holiness cannot cohabitate. "For the wages of sin is death, but the free gift of God is eternal life in Christ Jesus our Lord" (Rom. 6:23). What we have earned for our disobedience, what we deserve, is spiritual death—eternal separation from God. He cannot even look upon our sin, yet his love for us transcends our sinful state. "But God shows his love for us in that while we were still sinners, Christ died for us" (Rom. 5:8).

God knew that humans were not capable of living sin-free lives. Only God is holy. Only God is perfect. From the beginning, God had a plan to send his Son, Jesus, to provide a means of restoration—a provision to save us from eternal death. God sent Jesus to be born of a virgin in a humble stable—yes, the classic Christmas scene we so often take for granted. This Jesus, the Son of the Living God, who was God himself in the flesh, lived on earth as the only perfect human. He was a man without sin. As an adult, Jesus began to teach truths about his Father, God, but the day came for his great sacrifice for us. He was crucified on a cross to take that punishment of death that each one of us deserves.

"For God so loved the world, that he gave his only Son, that whoever believes in him should not perish but have eternal life" (John 3:16). Have you ever seen those signs along the roadside or in the crowd at a football game? Quarterback Tim Tebow even put "John 3:16" on his blackout strips below his eyes. That's because if there is one verse in the Bible you need to know, this is it. Jesus died so we don't have to.

The really cool part is that Jesus didn't stay dead. He proved his power over both sin and death by rising from the dead on the third day after his crucifixion and appearing to many people. His well-documented resurrection also proved that he is God.

So what is your part? What do you do? "If you confess with your mouth that Jesus is Lord and believe in your heart that God raised him from the dead, you will be saved" (Rom. 10:9). You must not only acknowledge who Jesus is and what he has done for you but also believe. Now belief is no small matter. After evaluating the facts, you have a life-changing decision to make.

Are you going to trust your life and your eternity to what Jesus did for you?

I have often used the illustration of a chair. I can walk into a room, dog-tired after a long day, and look around for a place to rest. I see a soft, comfy recliner in the corner, and I know it will provide me with the rest I need. I see that it is structurally sound, and I know it will not collapse under the weight of my tired body. However, that chair does me absolutely no good if I do not cross the room and rest my tired body in that strong padded frame. It is the same with Jesus. You can know what he did and the peace he offers, but believing means that you rest your life in his secure arms. You trust him with your life now, and you trust him with your eternal future as well. Is it really that easy? Yes! Yes, it is! "For by grace you have been saved through faith. And this is not your own doing; it is the gift of God, not a result of works, so that no one may boast" (Eph. 2:8–9). Jesus did the hard part. Faith is your part.

If you want to rest in Jesus's arms today, let me suggest this simple prayer for you to offer as you begin your walk of faith:

> Father God, I confess to you that I, like everyone, am a sinner. I have lived to please myself rather than to please you. Please forgive me.

Thank you for loving me and making provision for me, even before I knew I needed you. Thank you for sending Jesus to die and rise again on my behalf. I am trusting you today with my life. I want to rest my life in your arms, and I want to trust you with my eternal future. Please guide me, and help me walk according to your ways. In the name of Jesus, I pray. Amen.

If you have prayed that prayer, there is one more verse I want to share with you. In the next days, you may have doubts about the simplicity of God's plan. You may wonder if you really are the recipient of eternal life. God anticipated your questions when he instructed John to write these words: "I write these things to you who believe in the name of the Son of God, that you may know that you have eternal life" (1 John 5:13).

Believe it! Rest in it! You are loved! When you rest in Jesus, he is your Warm Place in the Sun.

Chapter 1

Joy on the Ugly Days

Memories of that day still haunt me—the day we took my sweet, Alzheimer's-ravaged daddy to the nursing home. Many books, movies, and TV shows have portrayed Alzheimer's patients and their families. They attempt to depict families doing life while a member of the family suffers the effects of dementia. I've watched them, read them, and sympathized with the fictitious characters, but it wasn't until my own father suffered from the disease that I knew the truth. All those shows, movies, and books terribly romanticized an extremely ugly disease. It's an ugly disease that leads to many ugly days.

At first, most people didn't realize Dad struggled with memory loss. He would ask the same question a few times or repeat a story over and over like most elderly do, but he seemed to function well. After a while, because of his own concern, he and Mom decided to get him tested, and the results confirmed his fears—Alzheimer's. After a couple of years, my husband, Chuck, and I realized that life was getting a little difficult for Mom to handle on her own.

Dad was having other physical issues in addition to the dementia, and Mom was supervising doctors' appointments and even driving him to the emergency room on occasion. I had no way of knowing how sick Dad really was, but we could tell that Mom was somewhat overwhelmed. Dad could no longer help with household chores without supervision, so all that fell on Mom. We were concerned but didn't know what to do. Chuck and I lived in Houston, Texas, and my parents lived in Phoenix, Arizona, which felt like the other side of the earth. I tried to get out there every six months or so to visit, but that just wasn't enough to satisfy my desire to take care of them.

I have always had a special relationship with my mom's sister, Aunt Loie. She is fun, silly, and loves to cook, but most of all, she is a very wise, godly woman.

"I need to call Aunt Loie," I told Chuck. As I poured out my heart and my concerns to Aunt Loie, she just listened. Toward the end of the conversation, I reached the real issue without even realizing it.

"I just wish they lived here by us," I said. "I want to be able to take care of them, take them to doctors' appointments, listen to the doctors, and help them understand. I don't want Mom to carry the load all by herself. I want to help."

"Let's pray about that," was Aunt Loie's matter-of-fact response.

"I can't imagine that they would be willing to leave a place where they have been for so long," I told her. "They have their church home and their doctors, friends, and family. I just don't see them making that kind of a move."

"Well, let's pray about that"—again, her only reply.

After a few more minutes, we said our goodbyes, and I went into Chuck's office to give him a recap of the conversation. "Well, they should move *in* with us, not just near us," Chuck responded. We just put an offer on a house that has plenty of room for them, too." (Coincidence? I think not!) "You should call them and ask."

"Like now? Like call them right now?"

"Why not?"

I called. "Hey, Mom, how's it going?" After the usual banter, I took a deep breath, gathered my courage, and asked, "So, Mom." I paused to reinforce my resolve. "Do you think you and Dad would ever consider moving here to live with us?" There was a long silence, and I could hear my heart beating.

"Well," she finally spoke, "under the right circumstances, I suppose we might."

"Okay," I said. A flicker of hope. "What kind of circumstances?"

"Well, if your dad passed away and I was all alone, or if he got to the point I couldn't take care of him myself anymore, I would think about it then."

I was encouraged, so now I got really bold. "Well, let me ask you this. Would you pray about the possibility of doing it *now*? I know you have a heavy load on you with Dad, with taking care of the house, going to all his doctors' appointments, and going to your own doctors' appointments. Chuck and I have talked about it, and we really want you to come. It would be our privilege to take care of you. We just put an offer on a house that has plenty of room for all of us."

"Oh," she said, somewhat stunned. "Really? Well, I'll talk to Dad, and of course, we will pray about it."

Whew! What a relief! I'm not sure what I expected, but I did *not* expect such a positive response. The next day, I got the following e-mail from Mom:

Things to think about:

Would we be able to contribute toward house, electric, and so on?
How long do you have to reside in Texas before you can register to vote? [Register to vote? Really, Mom? That's what you're thinking about?]

We have our niche purchased and our cremation paid for. Could that be transferred? I will have to make a couple phone calls on that. [She's so practical!]

Healthcare. What plans are offered? Anything with advantage program, although I've heard those are going to be done away with. [Again, so practical!]

Could we bring our car? It would give us a measure of independence until it breaks down. Then when it needed major repairs, we would just get rid of it. [Yes, she is extremely independent.]

We have been in this little condo 12 years. We have never lived anywhere else for that long. If you don't know, I like a change of place and space, so my mind has been many places on many things. [No, Mom, I didn't know.]

It is so good and kind and loving of you to offer us your home and heart. And we love you for it. In a way, I feel this is God's leading and provision for us. It would be hard for Dad to learn new places. A while back, we thought of changing the side of the bed we each slept on (due to some aches and pains) and decided not to change because he would possibly stumble around looking for the bathroom. Yet we know it will only get worse, so better now than later.

Lord, guide us and help us all is my prayer.

Love, Mom

"Read this! Read this! I think they're coming," I screamed, running into Chuck's office.

I spent the day researching and finding the answers to all of Mom's questions. I e-mailed her back the next morning. That very afternoon, she called. "Dad's on the other line." (They still used landlines.)

"Okay." I waited.

"Are you really serious about us moving in with you?" Mom began.

"Yes," I affirmed.

"Please tell Dad what you told me the other day," she added.

"Dad, Chuck and I would love to have you come and would consider it a privilege to have you in our home. We believe it is our God-given responsibility to take care of you as you age and as your disease progresses. I want to be able to take you to doctors' appointments and help you understand all that is going on. I want to be at peace knowing you are getting the best possible care. I want to be able to take care of Mom even after you're gone. We would consider it an honor, and it would be our joy if you would come."

"Tell Karen what you wanted to say," Mom said to my dad.

Silence.

"He can't talk," my mom finally said. "He's crying. Yes, we'll come."

There were many sweet days together once Mom and Dad moved in. I took them to appointments, and we went out to lunch together. I even took Dad shopping for Mom's Christmas and birthday presents. I have many sweet memories of those four years with Dad in our home. There were also some ugly days I prefer not to remember as Dad's disease progressed.

The nursing home day was one of the ugliest. After weeks of agonizing prayer, family discussions, conferences with doctors, and searching for the right place, we arranged to place my dad in a skilled nursing facility. "His disease will kill your mother," the doctor told me. I was forced to choose between what was best for my mom and what was best for my dad. No daughter should ever have to make that choice. You see, the problem was that Dad still knew Mom. He didn't know how to brush his teeth anymore, but he knew his wife. He knew her, and he knew she would help him brush his teeth. In fact, he knew she would help him get dressed, communicate, eat—everything. She was his lifeline, and little by little it was killing her. I tried to help him, but he only wanted Mom.

Well, the day came. We had chosen the place and arranged the time. Poor Dad thought he was just going to one of his many doctors' appointments. Upon our arrival at the facility, we were escorted to a large consult room. Mom sat next to Dad, and I sat across from them. A nurse stood to Mom's right, and a doctor was on Dad's left. As Dad looked around the sterile gray room and at the doctor and nurse on either side of him, his agitation grew. I could almost see his thoughts on his confused face. Who are these strange people? Why am I here?

Trembling inside, I began to explain the situation to my perplexed father. When he realized he was supposed to stay in this strange place without Mom, he began to shake with fury. How could his wife abandon him like this? Didn't she love him anymore? What had he done wrong? How can you even consider leaving me here? He refused to stay. As he began to express these thoughts, his voice rose. I tried to stay calm and explain. All the reasoning, heart-wrenching pleading, and tears went on for more than an hour. Eventually, I found myself raising my voice to my own father. I had never even done that as a teenager.

"You have to stay," I sternly told him. "Mom isn't strong enough to take care of you anymore. We have prayed and prayed about it, asking God what we should do. We are confident that this is what God wants."

I was praying that the Holy Spirit would touch that deep faith that I still believed existed in Dad's spirit.

"You've prayed about it?" he challenged.

"Yes, we have," I said. "This is what God told us to do."

"Well, God hasn't told me that," he yelled. "I'll pray. I'll ask God, and I promise you he won't tell me the same thing."

Through my tears, I said, "Pray about it, Dad. You pray about it."

"I will. I'll pray about it right now. I'll pray. I'm going to pray."

"Pray then, Dad. Pray."

Suddenly, he became quiet. His countenance changed, and he began to cry.

"Dad?"

"God just touched me on the shoulder and told me it's okay, so I'll stay tonight."

God had just given us a miracle. If God wanted Dad to stay, then that's what he would do, even if he didn't want to. And he most definitely did not want to.

We quickly embraced and said our goodbyes before he could change his mind, and the nurses and doctor took over. As we stepped into the parking lot, Mom and I collapsed into each other's arms and shook as we sobbed. My precious husband enveloped us both in his arms and prayed, this time out loud. I am confident that his silent prayers had sustained us all for the last hour and a half.

Yes, it was a very ugly day. There were many more ugly days to follow, but at the memory of that particular day, my stomach still churns. Some people call them trials, some tests. Some call them struggles, but that day was just plain ugly.

We all have them. Ugly days, trials, struggles, whatever you choose to call them, but they are inevitable as long as we walk on this fallen earth. So where was the joy in that struggle, that ugliest of days? In the cold darkness, where was the warmth of God's love? It was in the miracle that we witnessed as God spoke directly to my dad's diseased brain and gave him peace. It was in the confirmation that miracle gave me that we had made the right decision. It was in the family bonds along with the support from my strong husband.

You may not see the joy in your struggle today. You may be suffering through a series of ugly days, weeks, or even months. Take heart, my friend. God has not forgotten you. You may not feel the warmth of God's love, but keep searching. We don't find what we're not looking for. Jesus said, "Seek, and you will find" (Matt. 7:7).

> *Because he has his heart set on me,*
> *I will deliver him;*
> *I will protect him because he knows my name.*
> *When he calls out to me, I will answer him;*
> *I will be with him in trouble.*
> *I will rescue him and give him honor.*
> —Ps. 91:14–15 CSB

Set your heart on God. Immerse yourself in his Word. Find spiritual support in a Bible study group. Worship with a body of believers where you will be challenged and encouraged. Let's keep seeking. We will find joy in our struggles, and we will experience the warm glow of God's never-ending love.

A few years ago, I was seeing a counselor to work through some personal issues in order to understand myself a little better. You know, like why do I eat so much? Or why do I always want to be in control? Just a couple of minor things like that. Okay, maybe not so minor. Anyway, during one of those sessions, the counselor asked, "Karen, what is your favorite passage in the Bible?"

Without hesitation, I answered, "James chapter one."

"James one?" he laughed. "Your favorite passage is about going through trials?"

Well, we hashed through that one for a bit. I think he thought I was a sadist, or is it a masochist? (I always get those two mixed up.) The fact is, I've had lots of trials in my life, and I turn to James time and again. We all have trials, struggles, and ugly days. Whatever term you choose, they are painful. But there's good news! God tells us in James that we can have joy in our struggles because we know that God is at work building character in us.

Consider it a great joy, my brothers and sisters, whenever you experience various trials, because you know that the testing of your faith produces endurance. And let endurance have its full effect, so that you may be mature and complete, lacking nothing.
—James 1:2–4 CSB

Let's take a closer look. The word *joy* in Greek can also be translated "gladness" or "merriment." It almost sounds like we are to have fun as we encounter the trial, but to me, the so-called fun comes in seeing God at work. As we witness him at work in our lives and in our circumstances, we can be encouraged and motivated to trust him. We will be expectantly waiting to see what he is going to do next. When I am focused on my pain or difficulties, I don't see his hand. I don't find joy, fun, or anything pleasant when all I can see is my own suffering. Lift up your eyes, friend. Look around you, and see what God is doing in your circumstances and in your life.

Moving on to the word *trials*, we find it translated as "tests" or "temptations." The word *testing* means "proving." That means our ugly days can be a result of temptation in our path or difficult circumstances. Either will give us opportunity to prove our depth of faith, commitment, and dependence on God. I confess that I have never liked tests—the kind in school and definitely not the ones life brings. Your test—your dark, ugly day or situation—may be your opportunity to grow closer to God and be used by him in some unexpected way. Our trials can be adventures that we embrace with the expectancy of witnessing God's amazing work in our lives and circumstances. I have failed many of life's tests that God has allowed, but when we live expectantly, watching for God to do his work, we get to experience the joy of spiritual growth and the victory of "passing the test."

Endurance can be translated as "perseverance," that force within us that keeps going when everything and everyone says, "Give up!" So often I have wanted to give up, wave the white flag of surrender, and say, "I just can't do this anymore. Let me please rest, God." Yet in his faithfulness, God continues to uphold me and strengthen me until the trial has passed. That experience of his sustaining power gives me confidence in him to see me through the next trial.

It is just like exercise or weight training (not something I enjoy). If we consistently work out or exercise, our bodies become conditioned. I remember the first time I ever got on an elliptical machine. My thighs thought I was bat crazy and convinced me after 10 minutes that I had to stop or they would go on strike. Years later, my thighs may still complain after a while, but I have learned that my body is capable of 30 minutes or more on the machine of torture. Difficult or painful does not mean unable. It just means we need to build our endurance.

Perfect in this passage means "full, complete, or mature," and *result* means the effect. The endurance we are gaining by exercising our faith brings complete results—complete in every respect. Our physical workout produces endurance, but it also produces a conditioned body with toned and strengthened muscles. Our spiritual endurance produces toned and strong spiritual muscles that are well prepared for the next struggle, the next trial, or the next temptation.

When I plugged in these meanings, I came up with this enhanced, paraphrased version:

Consider it great joy, *gladness, merriment,* my brothers and sisters, whenever you experience various trials, *tests, or temptations,* because you know that the testing *or proving* of your faith produces endurance. And let endurance *or perseverance* have its full, *complete, mature* effect *or result* so that you may be mature and complete, *whole, perfect, complete in every respect,* lacking nothing.

"Well, I'm not lacking anything," you may say. "I don't need any more trials, and I certainly don't need an ugly day." I hear you, and I wholeheartedly agree. From my perspective, I have had enough ugly days to last me the rest of my life. I'm sorry to have to tell you that the trials won't stop coming until we see heaven.

Notice James's wording. It is not a question of *if* we will have those trials, but *when.* It's not as if we can avoid them. In reality, we are all encountering some type of struggle almost daily. Some of them are short-lived; others last a lifetime.

Joy—okay, how does that work? If I am going to struggle through this life, then where does the joy part come in?

Let's clarify. "Count it all joy" does not mean "Woo hoo! I'm going through a trial" or "Woo hoo! I'm unemployed" or "Woo hoo! I have cancer." God would never ask that of us. He created us to have deep feelings. Without our feelings of despair, sadness, or pain, we would not need to turn to our Heavenly Father for comfort and strength. "Count it all joy" means "Woo hoo! Jesus is walking with me through this trial. Woo hoo! I'm going to see God at work in my life. Woo hoo! I am not alone."

My joy on my ugliest day came from knowing that God had given clear direction and that I should stay the course. Joy came from being thankful that he had not abandoned me in my time of need. I found joy knowing he had given me wisdom and strength. There was joy feeling his presence and witnessing the miracle of his hand on Dad's shoulder and quiet voice in his ear. Joy filled me as my husband supported, prayed, and embraced us. Sometimes, the joy or happiness comes when we look back on the trial, but it comes.

Have you ever been happy and sad at the same time? I remember when God called my husband and me to be missionaries. We were saying goodbye to our precious church family who had nurtured us, witnessed our call to ministry, and trained us. We had been part of Trinity Baptist Church in Vacaville, California, for 10 years. The relationships were deep and precious to us, yet it was time to move on. The church had a special sending off service for us with a reception afterward. I cried a river that day saying goodbye to all those sweet people and hugging their necks in the receiving line. Yet I was filled with joy and excitement over a new adventure and all that God had for us in a new place. I was sad. I was happy.

There are those who teach that joy and happiness are two different things, yet I personally have difficulty separating the two. As I study the words, I find little difference in applications in the Bible. Some say that joy is the inner peace and knowledge that God is in control in a difficult situation. While that is true, I assert that this same knowledge makes me happy. I rarely have one emotion at a time. Sometimes, I am excited while fearful. Often, I am nervous while hopeful. In my struggles, I am frequently discouraged, sad, or angry while at the same time joyful or happy that God is in control. "I will not leave you or forsake you" (Josh. 1:5b). In Vacation Bible School in the fourth grade, I made a plaster of Paris plaque with that verse on it. Those words made an impression on me then, and I still hang on to them now.

What is your struggle today? Perhaps it is a long-term illness or chronic pain that is wearing you down. It may be the loss of a loved one or maybe the painful process of losing a loved one to dementia or cancer.

That kind of grief can bring you to your knees without the strength to even lift up a prayer. What about divorce or a custody dispute? Rejection, opposition, or a rebellious child—they all can provide many an ugly day. Maybe for you it's work stress, financial stress, unemployment, or homelessness.

You may be experiencing more than one of these struggles today or even some other type of trial. I want to gently remind you that God is your source. He is your source of comfort. He is your strength. He may not change your circumstances today, but he can and will enable you to endure and rise above your circumstances.

Have you not known? Have you not heard?
The Lord is the everlasting God,
    the Creator of the ends of the earth.
He does not faint or grow weary;
    his understanding is unsearchable.
He gives power to the faint,
    and to him who has no might he increases
strength.
Even youths shall faint and be weary,
    and young men shall fall exhausted;
but they who wait for the Lord shall renew
their strength;

> *they shall mount up with wings like eagles;*
> *they shall run and not be weary;*
>   *they shall walk and not faint.*
> —Isa. 40:28–31

I don't know what you are going through, my friend, but let me encourage you. God is trustworthy. His promises are true. Read them. Meditate on them. Let his truth and peace wash over you. Listen to his voice as he whispers, "I've got this."

Chapter 2

God Is Sufficient

So to keep me from becoming conceited because of the surpassing greatness of the revelations, a thorn was given me in the flesh, a messenger of Satan to harass me, to keep me from becoming conceited. Three times I pleaded with the Lord about this, that it should leave me. But he said to me, "My grace is sufficient for you, for my power is made perfect in weakness." Therefore I will boast all the more gladly of my weaknesses, so that the power of Christ may

rest upon me. For the sake of Christ, then, I am content with weaknesses, insults, hardships, persecutions, and calamities. For when I am weak, then I am strong.

—2 Cor. 12:7–10

Every time I read about Paul's thorn in the flesh, I wonder what it was that plagued him throughout his ministry. Many have speculated, but no one really knows. Some have said it must have been some type of temptation that tormented him throughout his life. Others have suggested that it was a physical ailment or pain, while still others pose the possibility of a speech impediment of some sort. It had to be something significant enough to make Paul feel weak and inadequate for the ministry to which he was called. All we know for certain is that he had to fully rely on God and the sufficiency of his grace in order to overcome his circumstances.

What is your greatest fear? What is your battle? What is that "thorn" that would cause you to struggle or even stumble? What is that one thing that makes you think, "I could never endure that. I couldn't survive that kind of trial"? Maybe you're going through it right now. Is it divorce? Losing your job? Bankruptcy? For me, it is the death of a child or grandchild. I simply could not endure that pain with my own resources. I would curl up in a ball and stop functioning.

In this era of terrorism and mass shootings, it is not unreasonable to think that the unthinkable could happen. I have three granddaughters in two different public schools. School shootings are happening at an alarming rate in our country. My daughter Bonnie is a high school assistant principal at yet another institution. With her responsibilities, she would virtually be on the front lines in a crisis or attack. There's my grandson who is a manager at a coffee shop, another soft target, as they say. Then there is my other daughter, Kelley, and her family who work in a war-torn Muslim country where they regularly hear bombs and gunfire and occasionally are on lockdown status. My fears are not unfounded. They are, in fact, reasonable.

God does not promise protection. That's hard. He promises to be with me and with my children and grandchildren, but he does not guarantee their safety. If he did, there would have been no 9/11 or Sandy Hook. There would have been no world wars, civil wars, or car accidents. So many sons, daughters, brothers, sisters, parents, and spouses have come home from wars in flag-draped boxes. Too many have never come home at all. The fact is that this is a dangerous world we live in, full of flawed individuals who at times make momentous mistakes. There is evil in this world that often goes unchecked. The consequences are grave, and we all pay the price. God has never promised that bad things won't happen.

How do we function within our fear without allowing its paralyzing ability to control us? It's in the part that says "for when I am weak, then I am strong." God is the strong one. God is the courageous one. He is the one who holds us up. I cannot be assured that nothing bad will happen to my loved ones, but I am confident of the one who will care for me in my greatest time of need. God's sufficiency means that he is the one who gives peace that surpasses all understanding. He is the one who brings comfort.

> Fear not, for I am with you;
>> be not dismayed, for I am your God;
> I will strengthen you, I will help you,
>> I will uphold you with my righteous right hand.
>
> —Isa. 41:10

God does not ask us to walk blindly through this life unaware of the threats and dangers around us. He was the one who warned Joseph in a dream that he, Mary, and the baby Jesus were in danger and that they should flee to Egypt to escape the wrath of Herod. God understands danger, yet he asks that we rely on him and trust him. I have to know that whatever happens, my God is enough. I am weak, but he will make me strong. He will sustain me. He will comfort me and bring peace.

How do I know that? I see him in the Bible time after time bringing comfort to the downtrodden and grieving. God sustained David after the death of his son. Did David grieve? Absolutely! But he survived and went on to lead the kingdom.

> *As for you, O LORD, you will not restrain*
> *your mercy from me;*
> *your steadfast love and your faithfulness will*
> *ever preserve me!*
>
> —Ps. 40:11

It was January 2018. I could hear that the phone call was serious. Chuck's face was somber and his voice hushed. "What's wrong?" I asked as soon as he hung up.

"Fred has stage four colon cancer. It's bad."

"What? No!"

We both began to cry, and from that moment, we began to pray for a miraculous healing.

To say that Fred and Chuck were close friends is a gross understatement. They were closer than brothers.

"There is a friend who sticks closer than a brother" (Prov. 18:24b). Chuck and Fred were those friends.

Their friendship began in March 1977 when Fred stuck his head in the doorway of the Sunday morning Bible study class Chuck was attending. "Is there a Chuck Oak in here? I'm supposed to take you up to the dressing area to get you ready for baptism."

Chuck had recently recommitted his life to Christ. He was about to be baptized since he had never done so when he made his profession of faith as a child. We were joining Trinity Baptist Church in Vacaville, California, as a young married couple with our 20-month-old daughter. As Chuck and Fred talked and walked to the baptistry, something clicked. God planted the seed that day for a 41-year friendship that would endure the tests of time, distance, circumstances, and heartache.

Fred was serving as the part-time assistant pastor and youth pastor at the church while he attended Golden Gate Baptist Theological Seminary in Mill Valley, California. The church was one of many in the San Francisco Bay Area that provided part-time positions to seminary students in order to offer experience as well as financial support.

Fred and his wife, Laura, were living in an apartment by the seminary more than an hour's drive from Vacaville. With all Fred's youth pastor responsibilities and activities, the weekend commute had become a bit grueling. Once we realized the situation, Chuck and I offered Fred and Laura our spare bedroom for the weekends. They would drive up on Friday for the youth events, stay until Sunday evening or Monday morning, and then head back to the seminary. There were many long evening talks as we each shared our hopes and dreams for the future. Before we realized it, Fred had become our spiritual mentor, and Laura had become our nutrition and health guru.

It wasn't long before Fred convinced us to help out in the youth ministry. The first Bible study I ever taught was for the 10th-grade girls. It was horrific! The next year, Fred enlisted us to be counselors for the high school spring break retreat at Jenness Park Christian Camp. There are a couple of memories from that retreat that stand out to me. The first memory is of Chuck and Fred running off in the dark night laughing like a couple of school boys after placing a large, empty, metal barrel in front of the door to the cook's cabin. Then came the sound of the barrel crashing over and Anna Standifer's voice booming out into the darkness. "You'd better run! We'll get even with you two!" The next morning, both Chuck and Fred were perplexed with the toughness of their pancakes until they discovered the cutout disc of paper plate that had been cooked inside.

The other memory is of Laura coming up to me and saying, "Do you mind if I ask you a personal pregnant? Oops!" She clapped her hand over her mouth and then continued. "I mean a personal question. Oh, I'm so sorry. I don't mean to pry. I've just been wondering."

Laughing, I responded, "Well, honestly, I don't know. I have a doctor's appointment next week to see what's going on. I've been having some issues." And so began an enduring friendship between two couples as Chuck and I planned for the birth of our next child. Yes, I was pregnant. I will never understand how Laura could tell before I could.

Fred graduated from seminary in May 1978. Within a few weeks, Fred and Laura were packed and headed to Hesperus, Colorado, to pastor a small church about 30 minutes outside Durango. Our daughter Kelley was born that October, and weeks later, Chuck and I and our two daughters were packed and on our way to spend Christmas in Colorado with our friends who seemed more like family.

Chuck and I both learned to snow ski on that trip. Laura babysat our two girls while Fred, Chuck, and I headed to Purgatory Ski Resort to spend the day on the bunny slopes. Well, actually, I stayed on the bunny slopes trying to figure out how to get up after falling time after time. Chuck and Fred went on to the blue slopes well before Chuck was ready. He took many entertaining spills to prove his lack of skill. Fred often told the story of losing track of Chuck at one point. He looked back up the slope in time to see a skier flying over a mogul, feet in the air, and landing head first in the snow. Laughing, he thought, "Man, I wish Chuck was here to see that one. Oh! That *is* Chuck!" We all laughed until we cried.

The following year, in December 1979, we returned, now with a 14-month-old and a 4-year-old. Bonnie still remembers Uncle Fred helping her learn to roller skate in the basement of their little church. After Bonnie had several discouraging falls, Uncle Fred tied a pillow to her bottom with a rope.

The small First Baptist Church of Hesperus was across the parking lot from the parsonage, a cozy little three-bedroom house with a wood stove that heated so well that at times, we had to open the windows for a breath of cool air. One afternoon while Chuck was outside playing in the snow with the girls, Fred came up to me. "Has Chuck figured out that God is calling him into ministry yet?" he asked, somewhat chuckling.

We had all seen the signs over the past couple of years. Chuck would ask questions about ministry or inquire about the education required. He volunteered to do hospital visits with our pastor and jumped at any learning opportunity. One day, after fulfilling his volunteer role of printing the bulletins on Trinity Baptist's old Multilith 1250 printing press, Chuck mused, "It must be really nice to work at the church." Then, shaking off his verbal thought, he turned to me, "But I guess everyone feels that way, don't they?"

"Um, no they don't." I simply replied, smiling to myself. God was at work.

I turned to respond to Fred. "No, not yet," I smiled. "I just keep praying, but I keep my mouth shut. I want him to hear it from God and not from me."

A few days later on January 1, 1980, Fred walked in on Chuck who was sitting alone on the front row of the sanctuary of Fred's church. Chuck seemed to be having a heated discussion. "I'll do this thing, but I'll hold you responsible for taking care of my family."

"Umm, am I interrupting something?" Fred asked from the back.

"No, God and I are just getting something straight. I just agreed to his calling to ministry, but I need to know that he will take care of all my girls."

Chuck and Fred spent precious time that day praying together and talking about the future. They had high hopes that God would allow them to minister side by side some day in some yet-to-be-determined place.

Fast-forward a few months after we returned home, and Chuck received a call from Fred. He and Laura had been fast-tracked by the Southern Baptist International Mission Board (IMB). They would be leaving in a few weeks for orientation and then on to Spain as missionaries. Wait. What? What about Christmas this year? What about serving together? Chuck had already resigned from his job and was full speed ahead with his education to work toward ministry. Trinity Baptist had hired him as their part-time assistant pastor with responsibilities in evangelism and missions education. This was more or less an internship while he completed college and seminary. Now with Fred and Laura on their way to Spain, it seemed as though the friendship that was more like family would be long distance from that point on. Chuck decided that if they couldn't do ministry together, he would at least be the best missions advocate he could be for his friend.

It was this advocating for Fred, Laura, and many other missionaries that brought Chuck to know and eventually follow God's calling to the mission field. Naturally, our first thought was to go to Spain to serve alongside Fred and Laura, but we knew we needed to go where God called and not just go where our friends were. We began to research different countries and overseas ministries while Chuck continued his schooling.

Four years later, Fred and Laura came back for their stateside assignment, as the IMB called it. The same little parsonage in Hesperus, Colorado, was their home base for the year as they traveled to various churches and conferences reporting on the work in Spain. Naturally, we were aching to spend time with our dear friends. We had also been invited by the IMB to attend a conference in Glorieta, New Mexico, to explore the mission career opportunities they offered. Since Fred and Laura would also be attending, we arranged to go to the conference and then spend additional time with them in Colorado.

We packed up our two girls and set off for the long drive from California to New Mexico. It was a sweet road trip for our little family of four with much anticipation of the conference and time with our friends. We knew that God was going to show us where in the world he was calling us. It was so exciting. After our arrival and check-in, we connected with Fred and Laura. They were eager to introduce us to all the other missionaries they served with in Spain. Their group latched onto us and loved us as if we were their own. Over the next few days, we attended breakouts sponsored by each area of the world. We checked out Asia, Africa, and various countries in South America. While they all seemed interesting, none of them were "calling our name." The last day, we met up with the group from

Spain for breakfast. "We're kind of hurt that you haven't come to one of our breakouts," Phyllis Baker spoke up. "You need to give us a chance."

"Okay, we're going to Santa Fe to be tourists with Laura this morning, but we will come to your breakout this afternoon."

Walking the streets of Santa Fe, we were fascinated by the sights, sounds, and Southwestern architecture. As we rounded a corner, we came upon the oldest church in the United States, San Miguel Chapel. We were intrigued and walked in through the enormous, carved, wooden doors. There from the back we observed the ornate yet primitive statues and carvings. In front was the large image of Jesus hanging on the cross. Then there were the people. Sitting just a few feet from us were a few women kneeling at the last pew, each praying and fingering her prayer beads. As we quietly eased our way back out, Chuck commented, "They just seem so desperate. It's so sad. In a place where they are supposed to find God, they look so hopeless."

"That's Spain," Laura said. "That's the perfect description of Spain."

God pierced our hearts, and a burden began to grow for Spain. We went to the breakout that afternoon and were captivated by the stories, pictures, and accounts of the ministry taking place among the countless without hope. God was calling us to Spain. It wasn't because our friends were there. It was because God, indeed, had a plan for us to serve there.

A few short years later, our calling was realized, and we went to Spain. There were difficult times for us, and a few difficulties arose for Fred during those years in Spain. In each of those hard times, Chuck and Fred were an encouragement to each other and cheered each other on. One morning, a very concerned Laura called Chuck. Fred and Laura had just moved to a different city to begin a new assignment. The change had been difficult for Fred, one that he did not want. He was angry and depressed. All their possessions had just been delivered in a huge, wooden crate the size of a freight container. It was sitting on the street in front of their house waiting to be unloaded. Fred could only sit on the front porch and stare at the huge box. He became angrier and more depressed.

"Chuck, I don't know what to do," Laura cried over the phone.

"I'll be right there."

Chuck immediately made a few calls, made a flight reservation, and arrived at their front door that very afternoon.

"What are you doing here?" Fred exclaimed.

"I heard you needed some help."

Fred welled up with tears as they embraced. While they worked together to unload the crate and get moved in to Fred and Laura's new home, the two men were able to talk. Fred began to process the changes and the assignment. They prayed together, joked around, worked, and talked. Two days later, Chuck came home.

"He's going to be fine," is all he said.

It was a friendship like no other. Later, God called Fred and Laura to another assignment in Norway where they thrived. Meanwhile, after three years in Spain, Chuck, the girls, and I returned to California for our one-year stateside assignment. We didn't return to Spain. God had called us to Texas. At that time, we didn't know what the future held for our little family of friends, but when the day came for Fred and Laura to return stateside again, our church provided a home for them. We were together again for a while. A few years later, when Fred retired from the International Mission Board, our church offered him a position. Chuck and Fred were actually working side-by-side in the same church for the first time.

A friend that sticks closer than a brother can also fight like a brother. Sometimes, Fred and Chuck argued, had a dispute, or hurt each other's feelings. It was all part of the deep love they shared. My friend Mark used to say, "They fight like a couple of school girls." There was even a dry spell when they didn't communicate at all. We had left the big church to be part of a church plant. There was quite an uproar over the few of us who left to start a ministry in a neighboring city. Many friendships were strained and some even severed. Chuck and Fred's friendship seemed to be one of the casualties. They didn't communicate for a few years, yet they still quietly kept track of each other.

I'm not sure who broke the ice first and made the phone call, but after a lot of prayer and self-examination by both, they agreed to meet for lunch. One lunch became two, and soon they were getting together every few weeks to share. During their time together, they began planning joint mission trips. They were then able to travel together to places such as Peru and Ecuador. The friends, these "brothers," were together again with a bond stronger than ever.

Then came the phone call, and the cancer journey began. They did it together. Chuck met Fred and Laura at the hospital or talked to them after every major oncologist consultation. He met them and hung out for every chemo treatment unless he was out of town on a mission trip. "I bring the party to the room," Chuck once told me. Instead of the dreariness of the hospital room, Chuck would reminisce with Fred, recounting story after story of their good times together. They laughed. They joked. They prayed. Week after week, Chuck traveled the 60-mile drive each way to spend the chemo day with his friend.

Fred was losing weight and deteriorating, in part from the chemo but also because his body was ravaged with cancer. Finally, after months of chemo and multiple hospitalizations, the decision was made to move Fred home and begin hospice care. We visited often, and at the end of each visit as we took turns hugging Fred, he whispered in our ear, "Please pray that God will take me soon. I just want to go home."

I have a picture on my phone that I took during one of those visits. I cherish it because it depicts the depth of Chuck and Fred's love for each other. Chuck is sitting in a chair next to Fred's recliner. Fred is holding Chuck's hand against his cheek, finding comfort from the presence of his dear friend. They sat like that for more than an hour without speaking.

Those were difficult days, yet God was faithful. He was sufficient. He made himself known. God gave us a compassionate and understanding pastor and church family who allowed Chuck all the time off he needed. They knew Fred was family. God gave Chuck grace, comfort, and strength to walk this journey with his friend. Even God's timing in calling Fred home was perfect. In September, as Fred entered the hospice stage, Chuck and I were due to go on a mission trip to Kenya.

"Don't come back," Fred whispered with vocal chords barely functional due to extended surgeries and intubations. He didn't want us to cut our trip short if he should go home to heaven while we were away. We, of course, knew that we would rush right back. As it turned out, that wasn't necessary. Fred was still there when we got home from Kenya. A few weeks later, we were due to go to Thailand on another mission trip. We were scheduled to leave on October 16. As Fred continued to decline, Chuck and I wondered if we should stay home. We were certain that he couldn't last until we got back. God quietly called Fred home on October 10. His burial and memorial service were held on October 15, and we left for Thailand the next day. Our God is amazing. He knew the timing we needed, but he also knew how long Laura needed to fight for Fred's life before she was able to reconcile with his death.

Chuck shared this scripture at Fred's memorial service. It's the same verses that Fred had prayed over Chuck at his deacon ordination 40 years earlier. It was their scripture.

I thank my God in all my remembrance of you, always in every prayer of mine for you all making my prayer with joy, because of your partnership in the gospel from the first day until now. And I am sure of this, that he who began a good work in you will bring it to completion at the day of Jesus Christ.

—Phil. 1:3–6

These verses were God's revelation to Chuck that brought him joy in the midst of his grief. Yes, he and Fred had a special friendship, and they were able to partner together in ministry for 41 years. God showed Chuck that his work in Fred was complete. Fred is experiencing his day of Jesus Christ. Chuck had joy as he remembered all the ministry and fun that he and Fred had experienced together. Chuck had joy because he knew his friend, his brother, was complete. God is amazing. God is sufficient. God brings joy in the midst of our grief and trials.

The loss of a loved one, anticipated or realized, can be crushing, filling us with sorrow, depression, and grief. You may have lost someone dear to you from cancer or some other illness or tragedy, but let me remind you that even in your grief, our God is sufficient. Not only is he sufficient to uphold you, comfort you, and sustain you, but he is at work to strengthen you and heal you. At some point, he will use that tragedy in your life for your good and for the good of others. Find joy in him, my friend.

Being strengthened with all power, according to his glorious might, for all endurance and patience with joy.

—Col. 1:11

Chapter 3

He's in the Small Things

Whether you are going through a major crisis or simply facing the day-to-day grind of a too-busy schedule and the never-ending "what's for dinner tonight?" know that God is in the small things around us. Sometimes, the small things are big things. I would call them miracles. If you need some encouragement today, look around you for a few moments, and reflect. What prayer has God answered for you recently? What little detail or blessing have you experienced? How has he provided for you? God is in the details and is at work even before we realize our own needs.

But, as it is written,

> *"What no eye has seen, nor ear heard,*
> *nor the heart of man imagined,*
> *what God has prepared for those who love*
> *him"*—

these things God has revealed to us through the Spirit. For the Spirit searches everything, even the depths of God.

—1 Cor. 2:9–10

My mother, who still lives with us, recently turned 90 years old. I wanted to do something really special for her, and since family is extremely important to her, Chuck and I planned a surprise birthday party for her. I told her that Bonnie and her family would be coming to spend the weekend for her birthday, which she would have thought very normal since her birthday fell on a Saturday. What I did not tell her is that my brother, sisters-in-law, nephew, niece, and their families were all coming from Phoenix. I also did not tell her that her sisters and some of my cousins from the state of Washington were coming, too.

I secretly shopped for all the food and then stored it in the garage. I ordered the cake and wrapped the gifts. The decorations were in the closet, ready to hang. I planned every detail, but a week before the party, I realized that the lawn service, which mowed our yard and a few others on our street, would be coming on Saturday morning just as all the family would arrive for the party. The lawn crew was working in the yard, but before I could get outside to ask them if they could come on Friday instead, they were gone. Not a mower in sight. Oh well, I thought. We'll just have to deal with the noise and the equipment next week.

The plan was to have Bonnie take Mom out shopping for a while on Saturday morning so Chuck and I, with the help of our granddaughters, could get everything set up, decorate, and start cooking the fajitas. We would have an hour and a half before Bonnie and Mom returned to get all the prep done and for everyone to arrive from their nearby hotels and Airbnbs. The only other problem would be all the cars. Hopefully, Mom wouldn't notice.

Well, Friday came, and so did the lawn service. God sent them on Friday, and I didn't even have to ask. And the neighbors across the street were having a two-day garage sale on Friday and Saturday. Yes! Mom wouldn't notice all the extra cars in the midst of garage sale traffic. I was filled with such joy. God knew about my concerns, and apparently, he just wanted to bless me. God demonstrates his love in so many little ways in the small details of our lives. We are often just too busy to notice. If we don't notice, we miss the joy.

There are times when we specifically ask God for something, maybe small or maybe not so small, yet the answer eludes us. It is so easy to ask but not always so easy to have faith that he will answer. Or maybe sometimes, we ask with the intention of telling him what to do rather than asking for his solution to our need or dilemma.

You do not have, because you do not ask. You ask and do not receive, because you ask wrongly, to spend it on your passions.

—James 4:2–3

Ask, and it will be given to you; seek, and you will find; knock, and it will be opened to you. For everyone who asks receives, and the one who seeks finds, and to the one who knocks it will be opened. Or which one of you, if his son asks him for bread, will give him a stone? Or if he asks for a fish, will give him a serpent? If you then, who are evil, know how to give good gifts to your children, how much more

*will your Father who is in heaven give good
things to those who ask him!*

—Matt. 7:7–11

God expects us to ask. He is our Father, and he
wants the opportunity to lovingly take care of us just
as a daddy wants to give generous gifts of love to his
child. Your Heavenly Father will not give you a stone
for bread. Give him a chance, and trust that he knows
what is best for you and your family. He is our provider.

Back when Chuck acknowledged God's call to ministry, he realized there was much schooling and preparation ahead. Since we had both dropped out of college
after we got married, Chuck would need four years of
college and three years of seminary. With two young
daughters, the undertaking was daunting. After a few
months of attempting to work full-time and go to night
classes at the local community college, he realized that
it was time to go all in.

After much prayer and under the leading of the Holy
Spirit, we decided to sell our house and rent an apartment
in order to cut expenses. The day after we came to that
conclusion, a stranger knocked on our front door. Chuck
was at work, so with Kelley in my arms, I answered the
door and was greeted by a sharply dressed, professional
looking woman with a portfolio tucked under her arm.

"May I help you?" I said.

"I hope so," she responded. "I am just finishing real estate training, and as I was walking throughout the neighborhood, your house caught my eye. Would you be interested in selling it to me? I want to live in this area, and your house is perfect. I would do all the paperwork, so there would be no realtor fees. How much would you want for it?"

There are times when God shows up in unexpected ways. This was one of God's little miracles that affirmed his calling and our decision to move forward to pursue that calling. Chuck resigned from his well-paid civil service position, became a full-time student, and worked part-time as a handyman. Shortly after our bold move, the church recognized the seriousness of Chuck's commitment and calling. They soon called him to join the staff. We used the equity from our house to pay cash for a new car, knowing that he would be commuting for the next seven years. The rest of that equity helped us make ends meet for a while.

Through all our prayer and seeking God's direction for this time in our lives, we both felt strongly impressed by the Holy Spirit that I was not to get a job until both girls were in school full-time. At that point, Bonnie was in half-day kindergarten, and Kelley was only two years old. We walked by faith that God would provide. After a few months, the equity from the sale of our house was gone, and our budget was tight. Bonnie was about to start first grade and had hit the first of many growth spurts. All her kindergarten clothes were way too small. There was no money to buy clothes, and my mommy heart was burdened. I prayed. I didn't really know what I expected God to do, but I laid the problem before him. I trusted. If my little girl had to wear tiny, tight clothes and short, short dresses, then that's what she would do. Almost as soon as I got up from my knees, the phone rang. It was our good friend Sandy.

"Karen, hi. I just cleaned out Melissa's closet, and I have some clothes here that she can't wear anymore. Would you be offended if we gave them to you for Bonnie?"

"Would I be offended? No! Are you kidding? We would be so blessed. Thank you!"

Sandy brought over two large paper grocery bags crammed full of hardly used dresses and outfits, and most of them were much nicer than Bonnie had ever had. My tears flowed as I pulled every little dress and jumper out of the bag, holding them up by the shoulders, envisioning my daughter wearing each one. I marveled at God's goodness.

Several months later, as Easter approached, I had already resigned myself to the fact that my little girls would not be wearing new dresses on Sunday. I knew that everyone would understand, and the girls seemed fine with it. The money just wasn't there. Another phone call. This time it was Shelba.

"Karen, you know I don't have little girls anymore, but I was out shopping and saw the cutest little dresses. I thought of Bonnie and Kelley, so I bought them. I hope you don't mind."

"Do I mind? Uh, no! Of course I don't mind."

Within minutes, Shelba was there with not only two precious matching dresses but also little white Mary Janes, tiny white gloves, white tights, and lacey hats with a big bow on each. The works! My mommy heart was full. God had given me a gift for my girls that I hadn't even asked for.

After three years of commuting to school, Chuck noticed that the tread on the tires of our only car was nonexistent. He was driving in all kinds of weather for more than an hour a day on bald tires. Naturally, there was no money for tires, so we prayed. If God can do dresses, he can do tires, right? Faith becomes a pattern. When you see God do something small, you start trusting him with bigger things.

Each day as Chuck set out for school, I prayed that God would keep him safe and that the tires would not slip, skid, or blow out. Then one December evening, the doorbell rang. We didn't often get visitors at our apartment, especially unannounced, so all four of us rushed to the door to see who it might be. Chuck opened the door as we girls craned our necks to see who was there. No one. Chuck opened the door wide for us to see. There, sitting on our front porch, was a stack of four big, black tires with a huge red bow on top. God is so faithful. Why do we so often doubt that he can or will meet our needs?

Therefore I tell you, do not be anxious about your life, what you will eat or what you will drink, nor about your body, what you will put on. Is not life more than food, and the body more than clothing? Look at the birds of the air: they neither sow nor reap nor gather into barns, and yet your heavenly Father feeds them. Are you not of more value than they? And which of you by being anxious can add a single hour to his span of life? And why are you anxious about clothing? Consider the lilies of the field, how they grow: they neither toil nor spin, yet I tell you, even Solomon in all his glory was not arrayed like one of these. But if God so clothes the grass of the field, which today is alive and tomorrow is thrown into the oven, will he not much more clothe you, O you of little faith? Therefore do not be anxious, saying, "What shall we eat?" or "What shall we drink?" or "What shall we wear?" For the Gentiles seek after all these things, and your heavenly Father knows that you need them all. But seek first the kingdom of God and his righteousness, and all these things will be added to you.

Therefore do not be anxious about tomorrow, for tomorrow will be anxious for itself. Sufficient for the day is its own trouble.

—Matt. 6:25–34

This was one of my favorite passages in those college and seminary days. We were living the reality of God's daily provision, and he most often did it through his faithful people. We never lacked for clothing, a meal, or even safe transportation. God is so faithful!

During those same years of Chuck's schooling, our church began a capital campaign. The pastor, staff, and leadership of the church believed God was directing them to eliminate the debt on the church buildings. This particular type of capital campaign was new and unique. The plan was for each family to financially prepare for one full year, saving up an extra amount equivalent to one month's expenses. At the end of the year, the families were to give every dollar they made that month to help pay off the church's debt and live off the funds they had saved. In other words, all salaries and any unexpected funds that came into the household that entire month would go to the debt retirement offering.

This was a huge commitment for our church family, but each family embraced the plan with enthusiasm and preparation. Our little family of four, however, had a problem. We just barely made ends meet from week to week. Saving money to get us through a whole month was out of the question. At the end of the year, we had enough money in the bank to pay our rent and utilities for a month, but nothing else. By faith, we paid those bills and gave Chuck's entire paycheck to the church.

Give, and it will be given to you. Good measure, pressed down, shaken together, running over, will be put into your lap. For with the measure you use it will be measured back to you.
—Luke 6:38

As the special month of giving progressed, God's faithfulness and the generosity of his people kept us in awe. Several mornings we awoke to find bags of groceries on our front porch. We received gasoline cards to keep our gas tank full, but every dollar, check, or cash that we happened to receive went to the church. During that entire month, we had no unexpected expenses, and our refrigerator had never been so full. At one point, we had five dozen eggs. The really amazing thing is that we were able to help other families out of our abundance.

That month, the church did, indeed, pay off its entire debt. The even bigger blessing was seeing the hand of God as he provided for his people and as they cared for each other.

Bring the full tithe into the storehouse, that there may be food in my house. And thereby put me to the test, says the LORD of hosts, if I will not open the windows of heaven for you and pour down for you a blessing until there is no more need.

—Mal. 3:10

God, indeed, opened the windows of heaven for us that month. It rained groceries at our house.

It seems so easy to doubt at times, but look around. Be aware. God is continually taking care of each of us, but we must look for him. He anticipates your needs. He listens. He will provide.

Chapter 4

Why, God?

If I'm obedient to God and serve him, why doesn't he bless me instead of allowing all these trials and struggles? For a long time, I carried a misconception about obedience and blessings. I thought that if I was a "good girl," God would bless me—he would give me good things and a good life.

I had a lot to learn.

Back when our family left California that first time for the mission field, we were filled with excitement and anticipation for all that God was going to do in us and through us. We arrived in San Jose, Costa Rica, for a year of language school, eager to learn as quickly as we could so we could get about the business of sharing the gospel. I had already studied Spanish in college and could read and write quite a bit. I was filled with images of teaching ladies' Bible studies in Spanish and inspiring women in their walk with the Lord. Upon our arrival, I was quickly jarred with the reality of living in a third-world country and the realization that I could not understand a single word that anyone said to me.

The first thing I remember was the smell. Every country seems to have its own scent. It wasn't an offensive odor; it was just different, a smell that said, "You are in unfamiliar territory." When we first arrived at the airport, a big bus met us and several other families destined for missionary service in Spanish-speaking countries. As the bus wound through the city streets, the sights and sounds of our new land mesmerized us. I quickly learned that the center stripe on the road was merely a guide, and cars were darting all around us, honking out of courtesy to let the bus driver know where they were. Such a noisy, chaotic place! One by one, the bus driver dropped each family off at their new home. We were one of the last families on the bus, and the anticipation grew as I saw each little house with its unique and primitive architecture. What would our home look like? How would it be furnished? Why are there bars on all the windows and doors? They all look like mini prisons. My thoughts were racing as we finally pulled up to the little house that would be our home for the next year.

With our abundant luggage unloaded and stacked high on the sidewalk, the bus pulled away. Chuck opened the giant iron gate to the carport and then the barred door. I took the first tentative steps inside and stopped. Oh wow! Red floors! I had red floors. I'd never had red floors before. Well, okay, I could adjust to that. My eyes moved to the dining table and hutch. Each wooden, black edge in contrast with the sepia stain gave the impression that all the pieces had been cut out with a wood burning kit. We found three small bedrooms, one small bathroom (with no tub, of course), a living-dining room, and a tiny kitchen that we cheekily called our one-bum kitchen. There was absolutely no way that two bums could move around that space at one time.

Outside the back door was a little contraption they called a washing machine. It resembled a large blender more than a washing machine. It could hold about one pair of jeans at a time and was filled by using the garden hose conveniently placed alongside. After the wash cycle, you had to pull the plug in the bottom to drain out the dirty, soapy water. A good refill using the hose completed the rinse cycle. No dryer, of course, meant we had to line dry the sopping wet clothes. The oven was fun, too. It was about half the size of an American oven and had one temperature—on. I actually got pretty proficient baking with it. I would sit on the floor in front of the oven and watch through the little window. If I thought it was getting too hot, I would turn it off for a while. As it cooled a little, I would turn it back on. I successfully baked cookies, cakes, and pies in that little "Easy Bake" over the course of our time there.

The first couple of weeks were filled with new experiences, sights, and smells. It was fun for a while. Then the culture shock crept in. If the red floors, washing machine, oven, and no bathtub weren't enough, I also had to go to church.

A time that normally should be filled with worship and refreshment was a time of confusion and frustration. Even though I had studied Spanish in college and even had an associate's degree in the language, I could not understand what people were saying. Some of the hymns and worship songs sounded familiar but frustratingly strange. It is one thing to learn to read and write another language. It is a whole other thing to be able to understand native speakers and, indeed, speak. I found myself so focused on the words I didn't understand that I missed the words I knew. If I did happen to understand a complete thought, my brain was paralyzed trying to respond. I spent so much time translating what I heard in my brain that by the time I had composed a grammatically perfect response, the moment had passed, and the conversation had moved on to yet another topic in which I was hopelessly lost.

One Sunday, we were horrified to find out that we had unknowingly insulted a precious church family. Apparently, two weeks before they had invited us to a Sunday dinner, but we had not understood. When you are learning Spanish and being inundated with words you do not understand, you tend to nod a lot and say, "Si, si." Well, we had nodded and said, "Si, Si" so much that we had accepted a dinner invitation without realizing it. The big problem was that we were not in town that next Sunday due to another obligation. (I think we were obligated to a weekend at the beach, I am ashamed to admit. We were desperate for mental refreshment.)

The day of the special dinner, the wife had gone to a lot of trouble to prepare the expensive delicacy—beef tongue. We were a big, fat no-show. It took a competent translator and many apologies to get us out of the doghouse with that family. (Okay, again ashamed, I did not regret missing the beef tongue.)

One hot afternoon, my language frustrations and culture incomprehension walked me right into the proverbial brick wall—grocery shopping. When we lived in California during Chuck's college and seminary days, my escape was grocery shopping. Weird, I know. Anyway, this was at the beginning of the true supermarket days, and there was a new store near us called Raley's. I loved Raley's. It had everything. It had a *lot* of everything. Raley's had the most amazing produce department and a deli right in the store. They even had makeup. I realize that this is the norm today, but in the early 1980s, Raley's was a phenomenon, my cherished phenomenon. If Chuck sensed that I needed a break, he would say, "Why don't you go to Raley's and browse for a while." (Yeah, he's a great guy.)

I share all this so you understand that when we got to Costa Rica in 1987, there was no escape at the grocery store. In fact, the grocery store was my most dreaded destination. First, I had to walk approximately a mile uphill to get there. Second, when I finally arrived, winded from the walk, there was no deli. There was no makeup. There was just food. There were hunks of raw meat and chicken with heads and feet still on them. There were vegetables and fruits I had never seen before. There were cans and boxes with words I could not read. There were a few snacks I could use for the girls' school lunches, like foreign-looking chips and something resembling cookies.

In California, we got paid every two weeks, so I shopped for groceries every two weeks and stocked up on everything we needed. In Costa Rica, we got paid once a month, so I thought I could go to the grocery store and stock up on everything we needed for the month—a month of mystery canned goods and surprise school snacks. I would walk a mile to the store, pile the oddly small shopping cart with food—only food—and then the bag boy would walk with me and wheel the overflowing cart a mile to our house to unload it and then take the cart back to the store. That mile walk home was one of the most painful miles of my life. There I was, a 30-something mom of two walking with a 12-year-old boy with whom I could barely communicate—walking in silence, awkward silence, for a mile.

My language skills were not progressing as I had hoped. On one particular shopping day, I wheeled my overflowing cart to the checkout counter, and the clerk rattled off a quick question. I gave her a glazed look of incomprehension. She rapidly repeated her question a couple of times, and I finally just shook my head in silent resignation. Then she laughed and commented to her coworker, "She comes in here and buys a mountain of stuff, and she doesn't even understand what we say." Sadly, I understood every word of that. I finally found out that she had been asking me if I wanted my groceries in boxes or bags. I was a shopping failure. I was the grocery store joke. The bag boy and I walked home in silence again as I fought back my tears.

A few weeks later, Chuck noticed that the pantry was getting bare and food was scarce in the fridge. "Uh, when do you think you will be buying groceries?" he asked. "We're getting a little low." I took one look at him, burst into tears, and went to bed. He hesitantly followed me into the bedroom. "What's wrong? What did I say?"

"I hate grocery shopping," I sobbed as I began to share my language and shopping frustrations with him. "And I miss my mom." Suddenly, all my culture, language, climate, and adjustment frustrations came pouring out. He hugged me, let me cry, and then encouraged me to rest. He also reassured me that he would help me as much as he could. But as much as he wanted to help me, there was little he could do. I had to turn to the one who gives me strength, but I was kind of mad at God. I had yielded my life to him. I had said yes to missions. I had left family and friends to serve him. Wasn't he supposed to bless me? Wasn't my life supposed to be filled with joy as I served him and did his will? Why was my life so hard? Why was I suffering? Where was the fulfillment of obedience?

Sometime during the night, God gave me a gentle yet not so subtle reminder. Was Paul's life easy? Was

Peter's? Was Jeremiah's, Isaiah's, or Jesus's for that matter? Paul was stoned, beaten, thrown out of city after city, and imprisoned a time or two before he was finally put to death. Peter was persecuted and died a martyr's death. Every prophet of God faced ridicule, suffering, and persecution. When did God ever promise that obedience meant an easy life? Where do we as Christians get this misconception? Jesus said, "In this world you will have trouble." Hello! Yes, that means me. That means you. That means all of us! But thankfully Jesus didn't stop there. He went on to say, "But take heart! I have overcome the world" (John 16:33 NIV).

God opened my eyes that day. He showed me that he was making me tough—tough enough to withstand the fiery darts of the future. He showed me that he was at work in the life of Zeidi, the sweet young single mom who came to clean our house every day while we studied language. Sometimes, the very fact that we are willing to suffer so that someone else may know about Jesus speaks volumes to observers we may not even know. He showed me that he was using my suffering to build character in our daughters who observed the endurance for the sake of the gospel. I didn't feel all that noble or worthy that day in bed with my tears, but God was at work.

There are times in life when we suffer as a result of doing exactly what God has asked us to do. The

examples in the Bible are numerous. The apostles were
beaten, stoned, imprisoned, and sometimes forgotten,
yet they counted it a privilege to suffer for the sake of
the gospel of Jesus Christ. They saw the big picture.
They were doing exactly what Jesus had asked them
to do.

Paul's life is an example of suffering as a direct
result of obedience to Christ's call to spread the gospel
of truth. Yet look at what he says:

> *I want you to know, brothers, that what has
> happened to me has really served to advance the
> gospel, so that it has become known throughout
> the whole imperial guard and to all the rest
> that my imprisonment is for Christ. And most
> of the brothers, having become confident in the
> Lord by my imprisonment, are much more bold
> to speak the word without fear.*
>
> —Phil. 1:12–14

What? Paul is in prison as he writes this, yet he is
seeing the positive results and the advancement of the
gospel because of his suffering. The guards are coming
to know Christ as Savior. Other Christians are being
encouraged and becoming more confident. They are
boldly proclaiming Christ. If Paul can do it, then we

can, too. Paul had spiritual eyes to see that God was at work in his own hardship. How often do we focus on ourselves and our own suffering instead of looking with spiritual eyes to see what God is doing in us and around us as a direct result of the difficult circumstances of our lives?

David is another example of someone who tried to live a life of obedience to God and suffered as a direct result of his obedience, work ethic, and integrity. In his early years, David was a diligent shepherd who defended his sheep against the elements and various predators, including lions. God saw David's heart and character. He chose David and had Samuel anoint him to be the next king of Israel. As David matured, he also became a great warrior for Israel. Still in his youth, David proved himself by conquering the giant Philistine, Goliath, with his sling and a little stone. King Saul was so impressed that he put David in authority over all the other soldiers of Israel. David's successes increased and, unfortunately, caused Saul to be jealous.[1] "And David had success in all his undertakings, for the LORD was with him" (1 Sam. 18:14).

In his jealousy, Saul decided that he needed to get rid of David and ordered that he be killed. David found himself hiding in caves to preserve his own life from King Saul's wrath.[2] Later, when David was king, he again had to hide out, this time from his own son who sought to take over the throne.[3] David had many enemies throughout the years and spent long periods of time living and hiding in caves, but he learned many valuable lessons in his cave days. We benefit from the lessons he learned even today as we read psalm after psalm of David's songs and prayers to God. Here are a few of my favorites:

> *For you are my rock and my fortress;*
> *you lead and guide me*
> *for your name's sake . . .*
>
> *I will rejoice and be glad in your faithful love*
> *because you have seen my affliction.*
> *You know the troubles of my soul*
> *and have not handed me over to the enemy.*
> *You have set my feet in a spacious place.*
> —Ps. 31:3, 7–8 CSB

My rock! My fortress! For your name's sake! Do you realize that every time we go through a struggle or dark time, God's reputation is on the line? Oh, he takes care of us because he treasures us, but he also draws attention to himself by demonstrating his power, his love, and his care for his children. When we rely on him, we give him glory.

He is your rock to stand on. You can rest in him and give him glory. He is your fortress. He has not handed you over to the enemy but rather has placed you in his safe place. Give him glory. His good name is at stake. You can trust him.

For you have been my refuge,
a strong tower against the enemy.

—Ps. 61:3

Have you ever visited an old fort on a historical battleground or seen the ancient stone walls that circle many of the older cities in Europe? Envision for a moment those aging stone walls that have endured spears, gunfire, and cannonballs. See in your mind those sentry towers that were built to carefully watch for the next attack. God does that for us. He is our citadel against the cannonballs of the world, shielding us from the arrows of the powers of darkness and even the IEDs of our own mistakes. We can take shelter in the truth of his Word, his promises, and his peace.

There are many psalms where David honestly cries out to God in his distress. He feels depressed and hopeless at times, but he also knows where to turn in his darkest hours. He knows that Jehovah God will listen. He knows that Jehovah God will answer the deepest aches of his heart.

How long, Lord? Will you forget me forever?
How long will you hide your face from me?
How long will I store up anxious concerns
within me,
agony in my mind every day?
How long will my enemy dominate me?

Consider me and answer, Lord my God.
Restore brightness to my eyes;
otherwise, I will sleep in death.
My enemy will say, "I have triumphed over
him,"
and my foes will rejoice because I am shaken.
—Ps. 13:1–4 CSB

David has no problem with honesty when it comes to his relationship with God. He pours out his frustration and pain with no filter. It's real. It's raw. What I find most interesting, however, is that in almost every psalm written from fear, pain, or discouragement, David regularly comes to a perspective of praise by the end of the psalm. The very act of crying out to God in distress, the mere communication, brings David back to an acknowledgment of who God is. Look at the rest of this same psalm.

But I have trusted in your faithful love;
my heart will rejoice in your deliverance.
I will sing to the LORD
because he has treated me generously.

—Ps. 13:5–6 CSB

Time after time, David found God to be faithful. He learned that God could be trusted. He learned that God was always his refuge. David's greatness was the result of faith through adversity.

Therefore let everyone who is faithful pray to
you immediately.
When great floodwaters come,
they will not reach him.
You are my hiding place;
you protect me from trouble.
You surround me with joyful shouts of
deliverance. Selah

—Ps. 32:6–7 CSB

Think about it for a minute. Who or what is your enemy? What circumstance, situation, or person has engaged you in battle? The same God who sustained David is also your rock and fortress. He is your refuge and strong tower. He sees your affliction. He knows the trouble of your soul and depression. Cry out to him. He hears you just as he heard David. Allow him to set your feet in a spacious place—a safe place. Trust him to hold back the floodwaters. Let Jehovah God, the God of all comfort, wrap his loving arms around you and sustain you.

Chapter 5

Trust His Plan

When you are in the middle of your dark, ugly day or trial, you can't see the purpose. There is no way Joseph understood why he was in prison, even as he learned his new leadership skills that God would later use. God took an arrogant teenage boy, allowed him to be sold into slavery and be falsely accused and imprisoned in order to humble him and build his character. God was preparing Joseph. God had a plan. His story is recorded in Genesis 37–50. Let's look at his journey together.

Joseph was one of 12 brothers from the ultimate in blended families. Jacob, the dad of the 12, had five sons with Leah, his first wife, and two sons with Rachel, his second and most beloved wife (while still married to his first wife). He also had two sons with Rachel's slave, Bilhah, and two sons with Leah's slave, Zilpah.

Of all the brothers, Joseph was Jacob's favorite, and he made no secret of it. Jacob even had a special multicolored coat custom-made just for Joseph. Naturally, all the other brothers resented Joseph and his jacket.

In Genesis 37, we see God begin to reveal his plan to Joseph in dreams. This 17-year-old boy couldn't comprehend the significance of those dreams, but God used Joseph's lack of understanding to fulfill his plan. Joseph shared the mysterious dreams with his brothers and gave them yet another reason to ridicule him and despise him.

> *His brothers said to him, "Are you indeed to reign over us? Or are you indeed to rule over us?" So they hated him even more for his dreams and for his words.*
>
> —Gen. 37:8

The brothers were appalled that their sheaves of grain had bowed down to Joseph's in the dream. As if that weren't enough, God gave Joseph another dream. This time, the sun, moon, and 11 stars were bowing down to Joseph. Now, even his father rebuked him. "Shall I and your mother and your brothers indeed come to bow ourselves to the ground before you?" (Gen. 37:10). No one seemed to like that idea.

Sometime later, the brothers saw their opportunity to be rid of this pesky, arrogant, younger brother. While they were tending their father's flocks at Dothan, Joseph came at Dad's request to check up on them. The brothers saw Joseph coming and huddled up. I can imagine them saying something like "Here comes that dreamer. Here's our chance." They began a plot to kill Joseph. Reuben, one of the older brothers, talked them out of killing him, and instead, they threw him into a pit. Reuben planned to come back and free Joseph later, but he was too late. While Reuben was away, the other brothers sold Joseph into slavery to a passing caravan. Reuben was horrified when he came back. Yet I imagine out of panic and desperation, he helped the brothers come up with a plan to deceive their father by telling him that an animal had killed Joseph.

Joseph's father, Jacob, was understandably devastated at the news and grieved deeply at the loss of his favorite son. Meanwhile, Joseph was sold to Potiphar, an Egyptian official, as a household slave.

The LORD was with Joseph, and he became a successful man, and he was in the house of his Egyptian master. His master saw that the LORD was with him and that the LORD caused all that he did to succeed in his hands. So Joseph found favor in his sight and attended him, and he made him overseer of his house and put him in charge of all that he had.

—Gen. 39:2–4

As slaves go, Joseph was doing well. It seemed that God was rewarding his work ethic and faithfulness with success. But then, Potiphar's wife became frustrated that Joseph, who was trying to live a life pleasing to God, kept rebuffing her physical advances. No woman likes rejection. She was hurt and offended. Her final attempt to seduce Joseph ended with his fleeing and her standing alone with his robe in her hand. She had been rejected one time too many. She took his robe and showed it to everyone. She told all her servants and her husband that Joseph had attempted to rape her.

Having no reason to doubt his wife, Potiphar had the expected reaction. With no trial or due process, he ordered Joseph to be arrested and thrown in prison, the same prison where the king's prisoners were confined. Joseph had to be wondering why God was allowing him to suffer for doing everything right, but instead of complaining, Joseph maintained his godly work ethic.

> *But the LORD was with Joseph and showed him steadfast love and gave him favor in the sight of the keeper of the prison. And the keeper of the prison put Joseph in charge of all the prisoners who were in the prison. Whatever was done there, he was the one who did it. The keeper of the prison paid no attention to anything that was in Joseph's charge, because the LORD was with him. And whatever he did, the LORD made it succeed.*
>
> —Gen. 39:21–23

If I had been sold into slavery by my own brothers and then later thrown into prison, I think I would be depressed and angry—angry with my family, angry with God, and angry with just about anyone else who dared cross my path. I am so inspired by Joseph's example. Are you in some kind of prison today? Do you feel trapped by your life and circumstances? God has not forgotten you. Please try to not be angry or depressed. Ask God to use this time as your training ground. Give God and those around you your best effort in attitude and actions. Just like Joseph, we don't know how long our time of so-called imprisonment will last, but we can keep our focus on Jesus. We can let him be the hope that will see us through, and we can trust that God is working out his plan. There is definitely joy in that.

God continued working his plan in Joseph's life with more dreams. Two of his co-inmates had their own dreams. By now, God had given Joseph a good understanding of dreams and how to interpret them, so Joseph offered his assistance. The king's chief cupbearer's dream indicated that he would soon be freed from prison and restored to his former position. Joseph asked that the cupbearer please remember him to Pharaoh once he was back on the job.

The king's chief baker also had a dream, but the interpretation of his dream was not so positive. His dream indicated that he would soon be executed. Both dreams were fulfilled, just as Joseph said, but the chief cupbearer got back to work and forgot all about Joseph.

God was not done with the dream revelations. Two years later, while Joseph was still running things down in the dungeon, Pharaoh began having dreams. He was quite agitated by them and sought out all the wise men and magicians of Egypt to interpret his dreams, but no one had a clue. The cupbearer heard about the king's dreams, and he finally remembered Joseph. He probably said something like "Oh yeah, there was this guy, this Hebrew in prison. He's really good with dreams."

The king sent for Joseph, and of course, God gave Joseph the interpretations of the dreams. The king had dreamed about seven skinny cows eating up seven fat cows, and seven thin stalks of grain swallowing up seven plump stalks of grain. Joseph told the king that the fat cows and plump grain signified seven years of prosperity and abundant crops in the land, while the skinny cows and thin grain signified seven years of severe famine that would devour anything left of the abundance of the previous years.

Joseph went beyond interpretation and suggested that the king find someone wise to oversee a conservation effort to store away a fifth of the harvest from the seven abundant years in order to provide for the people during the seven years of famine. The king saw something special in Joseph.

This proposal pleased Pharaoh and all his servants. And Pharaoh said to his servants, "Can we find a man like this, in whom is the Spirit of God?"

Then Pharaoh said to Joseph, "Since God has shown you all this, there is none so discerning

*and wise as you are. You shall be over my
house, and all my people shall order themselves as you command. Only as regards the
throne will I be greater than you."*
—Gen. 41:37–40

When we seek to walk with God, to please him,
to be used by him in our circumstances, people take
notice. Pharaoh saw something special in Joseph. That
something special was God at work in and through
Joseph. That something special was Joseph yielding to
God's plan and making the best of his circumstances.
Some of us are really good at the poor-me syndrome
rather than the God-is-good syndrome. Rather than
acknowledging God and attempting to be useful
to him, we choose to wallow in our circumstances.
Joseph sought to please God in every circumstance.
Due to Joseph's offering himself freely for God's purpose, many people were fed and many lives saved,
including his own family.

Family reconciliation can be tricky. There are some
that are instantly sweet reunions with hugs, kisses
and tears, but there are others with unresolved hurts
and harsh words. No one has a perfect family, but in
the power of the Holy Spirit, we have the capacity
to choose to forgive. We can choose to take the high

road and extend love to those who have been cruel, thoughtless, or unkind. Tragically, there are those today who have been sold into human trafficking by their own families. There are those who have been physically, sexually, or emotionally abused by those closest to them, those who should have been trustworthy and safe.

Only God can change hearts. Only God can heal a wounded soul. If you, dear friend, have been impacted by a tragedy such as these, I pray God's healing comfort over you and a spirit of forgiveness that will help free you from bitterness and bondage. While I do not believe it is ever God's plan for one of his children to be abused, I do believe that he can and will redeem the experience. Let him be the salve that heals your heart. Healing brings joy. Let's learn from how Joseph handled his unexpected family reunion.

Once the famine was in full swing, Joseph's family back home ran out of food, just like everyone else. Jacob heard of the food in Egypt and sent 10 of his sons to buy food. Fearing for the safety of his youngest son, Benjamin, Jacob kept him at home. In Joseph's absence, Benjamin had become Jacob's new favorite son. Poor Jacob had not learned from his mistake. When the brothers came before Joseph to request food, Joseph immediately recognized them, but the brothers had no idea they

were bowing before their brother Joseph in fulfillment
of his dream. Eventually, with all the brothers united,
Joseph revealed himself.

> *So Joseph said to his brothers, "Come near*
> *to me, please." And they came near. And he*
> *said, "I am your brother, Joseph, whom you*
> *sold into Egypt. And now do not be distressed*
> *or angry with yourselves because you sold me*
> *here, for God sent me before you to preserve*
> *life."*
>
> —Gen. 45:4–5

The brothers were terrified of Joseph's retribution,
but Joseph reassured them that he had no intent to
harm them. There were lots of hugs and tears and
finally even a reunion with his father, Jacob. In spite
of the sweet reunion, Joseph's bothers were left with
remnants of their guilt and shame. They were keenly
aware that they did not deserve Joseph's forgiveness
for all the hardships and cruelty he had endured as a
result of their hateful and hasty sale. Upon the death
of their father, all the fear of retribution returned and
caused them to entreat Joseph again for his forgiveness. Joseph's response in the midst of grieving for his
father shows his maturity and his faith.

But Joseph said to them, "Do not fear, for am I in the place of God? As for you, you meant evil against me, but God meant it for good, to bring it about that many people should be kept alive, as they are today. So do not fear; I will provide for you and your little ones." Thus he comforted them and spoke kindly to them.

—Gen. 50:19–21

Can you trust God's plan as Joseph did? Are you willing to forgive those who have caused you great pain, knowing that God has a greater plan that you may not understand?

Once Chuck and I felt God calling us to Spain, we shifted our general ministry preparation to a more specific goal of mission service in Spain. Chuck still had two years of seminary left, but his motivation had become even stronger. By this time, both girls were in school, so I took advantage of their school hours to enroll in community college where I began to study Spanish with purpose and vigor. We were Spain-bound. Or so we thought.

As we navigated the lengthy process of application with the International Mission Board, our focus remained on Spain. Once our applications, doctrinal statements, life histories, and personal testimonies passed scrutiny, we were given actual job assignment possibilities to review and choose. There was one request for Spain, and we latched onto it.

It wasn't until several weeks later, right before we were to attend Candidate Conference in Richmond, Virginia, that we learned that Spain was not accepting new missionaries. The Spanish Baptist Union was working through a dispute and would not approve our appointment. No one could tell us how long the delay would be—a few months, a year, or two. No one knew. There was an additional complication. At that time, the IMB had a policy not to appoint anyone with a child older than 12. Their reasoning was that the teenage years are difficult enough without moving out of the country, leaving friends behind, and learning a new culture and language. Bonnie was 11 and would turn 12 later in the year.

We had to decide what was more important, our call to missions or our perceived call to Spain. Even though I was somewhat shaken to think we had misunderstood God, we chose to move forward with mission service in a different country. Candidate Conference, our deadline for having an assignment chosen, was just days away, and we were feeling the pressure to make our decision. During the breaks at a marriage conference we were attending, Chuck and I found ourselves praying and pouring over each job description the IMB sent us. Dealing with feelings of disappointment and defeat makes it challenging to look toward an altered future with much enthusiasm. The marriage conference was giving us the balance we needed to stay positive and communicate our thoughts and feelings clearly to each other. In fact, we began to think that marriage conferences could be a future ministry we could pursue.

The stack of potential assignments was daunting. Since I had already studied and received my associate's degree in Spanish, it only made sense to look at Spanish-speaking countries, so we started there. We scrutinized each job description, but they were all very similar. How would we ever choose, especially since it seemed like Plan B? Then we came across a job description for an assignment in Coro, Venezuela. It was for a pastoral mentor who could also lead in marriage ministries and conferences. What? This must be it. We would have never considered Venezuela if God had not closed Spain. We were convinced that we were back on God's Plan A. We went to Candidate Conference on schedule, and two months later, in May 1987, we were appointed as missionaries to Coro, Venezuela.

We never made it to Venezuela.

After the appointment, we were sent to San Jose, Costa Rica, for language school. Upon our arrival, we became aware of other missionaries who were also appointed to Venezuela and had already graduated from language school but had not gone on to their job assignments. Apparently, the Venezuelan government had cracked down on visas for missionaries. Very few had been approved in the past months, and the process was taking up to a year. The IMB began our visa application process immediately, even though we were a year from completing our language study. During our time in Costa Rica, there were two families who ultimately received their visas to Venezuela. Two other families, after months of waiting, finally chose to go to another South American country.

Our graduation was approaching, and no visas had arrived for our family. The IMB encouraged us to stay in Costa Rica and work with tutors to continue language study while we waited for visas. A few months later, still waiting, we were told to return to California to continue our vigil. Months went by with no word or encouragement.

We prayed. Our family prayed. Our church family prayed. No one could understand why God was not answering our prayers. Why would God not answer when all we wanted to do was obediently share the gospel and encourage marriages in Venezuela? One of my close friends suggested that she and I go on a liquid fast for a week, confident that by the end of that period, God would intervene with the Venezuelan government.

We prayed. We drank our juice, and we prayed some more. Nothing happened. It seemed like God was silent. Finally, a phone call came. "You will have to choose another country."

"No!" I cried. "I can't do this anymore. We *knew* God had called us to Spain. We were wrong. Then we *knew* God had called us to Coro, Venezuela. We were wrong. If we are not capable of discerning God's will, I'm not going anywhere."

The next day, there was another phone call. Spain was open. Within weeks, our transfer was approved, our bags were packed, and we boarded a plane bound for Madrid. We went to Spain in August 1989 with a 14-year-old.

It can be confusing at times to follow God's will. It can feel like you are blindly navigating a maze or labyrinth of mirrors in a fun house (I never did like those things). The confusion can cause panic. We reach out trying to feel our way along each turn or detour with the little information we have, longing to find the exit to the game, to see the light and open landscape around us. Faith. Trust. It sounds so simple, yet it can be frightening not knowing the next step. This is where we must draw upon truth—the truth of God's Word, all we know of God's character, and all we know he has done in the past. He has proved himself trustworthy time after time. His promises will not fail. Even in your maze of confusion, he is faithful.

And we know that for those who love God all things work together for good, for those who are called according to his purpose.
                                                    —Rom. 8:28

It's not just the good things; all things work into God's plan. Does that mean it is God's will for others to treat us badly as Joseph's brothers did? No, but it is his will that we allow him to use those circumstances to grow us, to change us, and to use us for his glory. He has purpose even in allowing our pain. When we can't see God's purpose, we have to trust. Trust that God has a plan. Trust that God is sovereign. If he allows it, he will use it.

Chapter 6

Just Keep Showing Up

Our days in Spain were some of the sweetest and some of the hardest. "It was the best of times, it was the worst of times."[1]

We spent our first year in Spain in the magnificent city of Madrid doing more language and cultural studies to prepare us for ministry. The following two years, we went to the Island of Mallorca where Chuck was to pastor a small congregation. Up to that point, Chuck had never been a lead pastor. He had always worked under a senior pastor as an associate with primary responsibilities in missions and evangelism. He was a little nervous yet optimistic about taking the lead role. Lacking somewhat in his confidence to lead, he lacked even more confidence in his language skills. As pastor, he would preach twice on Sunday and again on Wednesday evenings, three messages to prepare in Spanish every week. He spent hours every week writing out his messages in Spanish to be sure they were correct.

Though lacking confidence in his language skills, Chuck did have confidence in his understanding of evangelism methods and opportunities. He had taught many classes on personal evangelism and participated in several cross-cultural evangelism training experiences. He had a knack for thinking outside the box and developing new opportunities to share the gospel.

Applying these tools in the church, Chuck immediately recognized an opportunity for relational evangelism. There were two women, each with teenage children, who attended Bible study and worship without their husbands. Chuck quickly discerned that their husbands were not believers and had no interest in things of the church. Without delay, Chuck reached out to each husband, attempting to develop a friendship.

One of the husbands, José Maria, was an executive for a Swedish hotel chain on the island. Chuck often drove across the island to visit him at one of the hotels where they would have lunch together. José Maria's wife understood what Chuck was doing and periodically invited our family over for dinner to facilitate the deepening of the friendship.

At the same time, Chuck found out that the other nonbelieving husband, José Manuel, liked to play tennis. Chuck became a tennis player. They met periodically to play and then have coffee afterward. As the relationship developed, we were often invited to Fina and José's home for dinner as well.

I was investing in the youth of the church. There was no other adult leadership for the group at that time, so in addition to teaching their Bible study on Sunday mornings, I invited the group over to our house on Friday nights, or we would meet in the park to play volleyball. The group continued to grow in numbers, and they were hungry to grow in their love for the Lord. It was a sweet fellowship, and Chuck often joined us in our activities.

By the end of our first six months, Chuck was preparing and preaching three messages a week, trying to spend time each week with José and José, offering evangelism opportunities for our congregation at the nearby neighborhood park, and supporting me by attending most of our youth outings and activities. About that time, the deacons of the church called a meeting and, of course, asked Chuck, their pastor, to attend. In the meeting, the deacons informed Chuck that he was not evangelizing properly and that they would no longer participate in his American style of evangelism. Their idea of evangelism was cold calling, literally knocking on doors with tracts in hand to share the gospel or preaching to complete strangers. It was all they had done, and it was the only way they wanted to proceed. Then they told him they didn't like him playing favorites in the church. They said he was spending too much time with the families of José and José. They additionally criticized his leadership style and sermon preparation and finally told him he was spending too much time with the youth of the church. He needed to focus on the adults. Chuck was blindsided, humiliated, and devastated. He came home from that meeting an empty shell.

Since our arrival on the island, one of the church members, Rafael, had offered to make notes and correct Chuck's language during the sermons. After each message, Rafael got together with Chuck and pointed out each error, big or small. He scrutinized and criticized each verb conjugation, vocabulary choice, and article. At first it seemed helpful, but after the meeting with the deacons, it felt vindictive. What Rafael didn't understand is that Chuck made mistakes in English, too. No one speaks perfectly in any language.

As you can imagine, Chuck's morale was extremely low, and his confidence diminished daily, yet he purposed in his heart to continue. "I'm just going to keep showing up, and I'm going to keep loving them," he told me.

As Chuck encountered his share of struggles and ugly days, I found myself also sinking below waves of adversity. In our second year of ministry in the Mallorca church, I began homeschooling our two daughters. The private British school they had attended the first year was not meeting their academic needs, and the environment was not one we wanted for our daughters. The mission board was generously paying an outrageous tuition for each of them, so we felt it prudent and wise to pull them out and teach them at home.

In addition to teaching our girls, I continued to guide the youth activities of the church. I led the music for Sunday morning worship, I taught an adult Bible study class on Sunday mornings, and I taught the women's Bible study on Thursday mornings. In my spare time, I cooked meals, cleaned house, and tried to support a stressed-out husband-pastor. If all that were not enough, I, too, had some unpleasant encounters with our church members.

One Thursday morning, our ladies' group had just finished our Bible study. As I packed up my Bible and notes, a discussion broke out regarding the schedule for cleaning the church. Our "local," as our church meeting place was called, was a small, ground-floor space in a five-floor building of pisos, or flats. Our local was divided into two sections, each measuring approximately 50 feet by 15 feet. One side was our worship center, and the other side was divided into a tiny kitchen, a small gathering area, and two Bible study areas, one for children and one for youth.

On this particular Thursday, it became apparent that among the eight ladies present, only six of them were participating in the cleaning rotation. I must admit that I was not one of the six. I had invasive back surgery just 12 months before to repair a ruptured disc, and no one expected me to sweep, mop, or stoop in any way. It was one of the few things I had not been asked to do in the church. So the eighth lady, Avelina, figured out very quickly that the entire discussion was directed at her nonparticipation in the cleaning. She was swift to defend herself, and sadly, the discussion escalated to an argument and finally rose to a full-scale screaming match between Conchita, the president of the ladies' group, and Avelina.

If you have ever learned a second language, you know that in a crisis, you can only think and function in your first language. Remember the old *I Love Lucy* shows when Ricky became so upset that he started spewing out Spanish like water from a fire hose? It was hilarious to watch but not so funny to live out. In this crisis, my Spanish was gone, but I was not even spewing English; I was just paralyzed. The ladies were screaming all around me. It was my job as the pastor's wife to "fix it," yet I sat silent as a statue with eyes and mouth wide open. Finally, one of the other women put two fingers in her mouth and whistled like a referee at a football game. There was sudden silence. Avelina then bolted from her seat and grabbed her coat as she ran from the building. As I describe this now, it seems as though it actually *should* have been something out of a comedy scene from *I Love Lucy*, but I promise you, it was far from humorous that day.

Not wanting such a disastrous end to the discussion, I ran out and caught up to Avelina in front of the building. While I ran, I was able to come up with a few words and thoughts in Spanish. We spoke briefly. She calmed down, and I was able to convince her to come back inside. She and Conchita went into the tiny kitchen and shut the door to talk privately.

After several minutes, I had to leave because I had a youth planning meeting scheduled at my home. I left, hopeful that a peaceful resolution would be found, but I cried as I walked away, feeling like a failure. I had failed as a pastor's wife to intervene and give spiritual guidance to prevent the screaming match. I had failed as a missionary to speak the language I had diligently studied, having to fall back on someone else's piercing whistle. I was humiliated and discouraged.

The next afternoon, there was a funeral at our church, an unusual occurrence for a congregation of 40 people. The father of one of our members had passed away. Many of the family members who would attend were not Christians, so it was a valuable and unusual opportunity to minister and expose them to the gospel. I was scheduled to sing a solo right before Chuck brought the message, so we both arrived plenty early to prepare. After running through my music, I saw Conchita enter the building and move to her usual seat in the worship center. As Chuck went to greet the arriving, bereaved family, I took the opportunity to touch base with Conchita.

"Were you and Avelina able to work things out yesterday? Are you two okay?" I asked.

"Avelina and I are just fine," came the cold reply. "It's *you* I'm angry with."

"But why?" I stammered. I was not prepared for the salvo that followed.

"As the pastor's wife, you should support me, the president of the ladies' group. But instead of supporting me and defending me, you said nothing. When Avelina left, you ran after her, but I needed you. You chose her over me. I was hurt and upset, and you abandoned me. You don't know how to be a pastor's wife. You say you love us, but you play favorites. You are supposed to love all of us. You say you love me, but you don't." And on and on she went.

From across the room, Chuck saw what was happening. He saw that I was being verbally battered, but he was helpless to come to my aid since he was comforting the bereaved family. Just as the verbal barrage stopped, the music for the memorial service began to play.

"Conchita, we need to talk."

"No, we don't," she said. "I have nothing more to say to you."

I turned to quickly sit down two rows in front of her, fighting the tears that fell and keenly aware of the hate emanating from behind me.

"How can I sing, Lord? I'll just signal Chuck to cut the song," I thought. "No, I will not give Satan this victory. God, please give me grace to get through this."

You should know that I am not truly a soloist. Although I have sung many solos throughout the years, I only have what I call a small church voice. I have never had the vocal quality or training to sing in a large church or venue, but I have managed to praise God and lead others in worship as the need arose. As I stood to sing, shaky from trauma rather than nerves, I felt God's arms around me giving me strength. I can tell you with total honesty that I have never, nor will I ever again, sing as well as the Lord gave me grace to sing that day.

After the service, with all the condolences and hugs, Chuck, Bonnie, Kelley, and I began our walk home. Chuck knew I was barely holding it together in front of the girls. Fortunately, they had been oblivious to Conchita's vicious lashing and were unaware of my wounds. We reached our building and rode the elevator up to the fourth floor to our apartment. As the elevator doors opened, Chuck said, "Why don't you girls go on in. I'm going to take your mom downstairs to the coffee shop for a bit." The second those big metal elevator doors met again, I collapsed into Chuck's arms, sobbing. He held me and let me vent all the hurt, tension, and despair I had held in for the last two hours.

We spent the next hour at our favorite coffee shop across the street from our building. Chuck was a great comfort to me that day. He could relate to my pain as no one else could. As we sat across from each other, our coffee getting cold on the table between us, I unpacked all that I was feeling. "I know Conchita needs to feel loved," I said. "But I don't know how I can help her with that. I have loved her the only way I know how, and it just hasn't been enough. God is going to have to love her through me, I guess, because right now, I don't even *like* her."

It was one of those crazy weeks in church life when something major is going on every day of the week. That Saturday's activity was the community prayer service. I didn't want to go. I knew Conchita would be there, and 24 hours was not enough time to recover from my wounds. I went anyway. We do what we have to do, right? Fortunately, Chuck and I had no responsibilities in the service. It was our church's turn to host, but another pastor and another worship leader were handling the entire service.

We slipped into the back row just as the service began. As the music started and the worship leader guided us from one song to the next, my focus was on the back of Conchita's head. She was sitting in the same seat as always, as I knew she would be, with her husband at her side.

"God, help me," I prayed. "Please help Conchita feel loved. Help her feel your love. Please love her through me. You know I can't do it myself. Let me love her with your love."

As I was praying, the worship leader began to lead us in the song "I Love You with the Love of the Lord." It's an oldie, and you may not be familiar with it. Here are the lyrics:

I love you with the love of the Lord,
Yes, I love you with the love of the Lord,
I can see in you the glory of my King,
Yes, I love you with the love of the Lord.[2]

Of course, we were singing in Spanish, but as I sang those lyrics, I thought, "Yes, Lord. That's what I'm talking about. It's not my love but your love that Conchita needs."

Just then the worship pastor said, "Now let's all walk around the worship center and sing this song to each other."

"You have got to be kidding me." Yes, that is exactly what I said to the Lord at that moment. I was almost angry with him. "Really?" But then I took a breath and submitted. He had given me an immediate answer to my prayer, so I had to obey. I made a beeline down the aisle to Conchita. I touched her shoulder as I sang. She turned toward me. Her shock was palpable, yet she looked at me, tears in her eyes. I sang that entire song to her, eyeball to eyeball. We were both weeping by the end. As I finished, she hugged me fiercely. Then a new barrage of words came. "Oh, Karen, I am so sorry. God kept me awake all night showing me how wrong I was. I know you love me. You love me well, and you are a great pastor's wife. Can you ever forgive me for how badly I treated you?"

The tears flowed, and the wounds healed with the salve of God's amazing love flowing through two imperfect women. As time went by, Conchita became one of our strongest supporters and advocates in a somewhat hostile environment.

There were many dark months ahead for Chuck and me, yet there was joy sprinkled in the struggles. We developed very dear friendships with the families of José and José. Those friendships remain to this day. There was also the sweet fellowship with the youth who truly had a heart for the Lord. And then there was the beach. Yes, we lived on an island. Isn't God awesome to give us something so pleasurable yet so simple in the midst of our trials? I love the beach.

To those not called to ministry, you may not relate, but there are many who have endured the same kinds of trials and worse. We must remember why we initially responded to God's call. It was simply to share the gospel of Jesus Christ and glorify his name. Sometimes, our joy comes merely from knowing we are obedient to that call.

Beloved, do not be surprised at the fiery trial when it comes upon you to test you, as though something strange were happening to you. But rejoice insofar as you share Christ's sufferings, that you may also rejoice and be glad when his glory is revealed. If you are insulted for the name of Christ, you are blessed, because the Spirit of glory and of God rests upon you . . . Therefore let those who suffer according to God's will entrust their souls to a faithful Creator while doing good.

—1 Pet. 4:12–14, 19

José Maria did kneel beside Chuck one afternoon in a private room in one of his hotels and pray to receive Christ. José Manuel prayed to receive Christ and was baptized a few years after we left Spain. That is *joy*! We spent two very long, hard years on that beautiful island, but our mantra became "just keep showing up."

Sometimes, staying in bed seems much easier than showing up to life. Trials come in many forms—in ministry and in everyday life. It seems the easy answer is to quit, to resign from that job, to end that relationship, or to just walk away. Sometimes, the joy comes when we stay and fight. I believe our time in Spain was one of spiritual warfare. Satan did not want us to be successful. He wanted us to give up and walk away in defeat.

Be sober-minded; be watchful. Your adversary the devil prowls around like a roaring lion, seeking someone to devour. Resist him, firm in your faith, knowing that the same kinds of suffering are being experienced by your brotherhood throughout the world.

—1 Pet. 5:8–9

So how do we fight this kind of battle? How do we resist the devil and keep showing up to the fight? First, we must acknowledge our weakness, just as Paul did when he spoke of his thorn in the flesh. Then we must use the armor God has given us so we can show up and fight.

Finally, be strong in the Lord and in the strength of his might. Put on the whole armor of God, that you may be able to stand against the schemes of the devil. For we do not wrestle against flesh and blood, but against the rulers, against the authorities, against the cosmic powers over this present darkness, against the spiritual forces of evil in the heavenly places. Therefore take up the whole armor of God, that you may be able to withstand in the evil day, and having done all, to stand firm. Stand therefore, having fastened on the belt of truth, and having put on the breastplate of righteousness, and, as shoes for your feet, having put on the readiness given by the gospel of peace. In all circumstances take up the shield of faith, with which you can extinguish all the flaming darts of the evil one; and take the helmet of salvation, and the sword of the Spirit, which is the word of God, praying at all times in the Spirit, with all prayer and supplication.

—Eph. 6:10–18

The devil most definitely is scheming against you as a believer. Your first step in the battle is to recognize the enemy. It's not your boss or your spouse. It's not your children, your crazy schedule, or your extended family. It's not the illness or loss you have experienced. Life always brings struggle and heartache, but our battle is against Satan, who would have us believe we are losers. *I can't win. I don't have what it takes. I'm always wrong. I'm not smart enough. I am too great a sinner for God to want to help me.* These are all lies from Satan who, along with his demons, wants you to quit rather than engage in the battle. They know that once we take up the armor of God, they will be defeated. Satan, beware! We are preparing for battle.

First, take up the belt of truth—truth, not lies. Truth is that God is in control. Truth is that God has power over Satan and over your circumstances. Truth is that God loves you and wants to hold your hand and walk you through this minefield of life. Truth is that God equips you. When Satan says, "You can't win," God says, "I have already won" (see John 16:33). When Satan says, "You're not good enough, smart enough, or don't have what it takes," God says, "I made you in my image. I formed you in your mother's womb. You are fearfully and wonderfully made" (see Ps. 139:13–14). When Satan attacks, rely on God's *truth*.

Next, take up the breastplate of righteousness. When Satan throws your past sins in your face, you must remember that Jesus's blood has washed you clean. Once you pray to receive Christ into your life, God makes you new. He makes you clean. When God looks at you, he does not see your sin; he sees the righteousness of Jesus that covers you as a believer in Christ. We can have confidence before Satan's accusations knowing that we are forgiven.

Next, our feet must be ready with the gospel of peace. God is peace. He is *your* peace. Part of the gospel, or the good news that Jesus came to redeem us, is that he also gives us his peace. God doesn't calm all the storms of our lives, but his assuring presence brings us peace as we traverse the rough waters. When Satan attacks you through your circumstances, you can stand firm in God's peace if you know the truth of his Word.

And the peace of God, which surpasses all understanding, will guard your hearts and your minds in Christ Jesus.

—Phil. 4:7

The shield of faith reminds you of all you know and believe about God. Faith and truth combine to protect you from the prowling lion. It is not enough to know about God and his might. You must believe it. Faith is more than knowledge. Faith is resting in the truth. Remember the chair? That cushy recliner of God's truth waits for you to yield your body into its comfy padding for rest. This resting in his truth is the shield of faith that will protect you from Satan's dangerous darts of deceit.

Salvation is our headgear. Your salvation, the fact that Jesus died on a cross and gave up his life on your behalf, is the protection you need for your brain. Experiencing freedom from condemnation of your sin and receiving the promise of eternal life are the weapons you should use to protect your mind from all the discouragement and depression that Satan wields in his assault. It is easy to allow our circumstances to dictate our frame of mind. When our thoughts are covered with the protection of our salvation, we can claim victory over negativity and despair.

The most effective means we have to use against this prowling lion is the sword of truth, the Word of God.

In this weapon, we have a reminder of who God is and of all his mighty resources. Reading it reminds us that he is all-knowing, all-powerful, and always present. He is unchanging, faithful, and kind. As we study God's Word and spend time with him, we get to know him more intimately and gain more understanding of his ways. It is through knowing him that we gain peace and grace.

> *May grace and peace be multiplied to you in the knowledge of God and of Jesus our Lord.*
>
> —2 Pet. 1:2

One of Paul's desires, even toward the end of his life and ministry, was to know God more.

> *Indeed, I count everything as loss because of the surpassing worth of knowing Christ Jesus my Lord. For his sake I have suffered the loss of all things and count them as rubbish, in order that I may gain Christ . . . that I may know him and the power of his resurrection.*
>
> —Phil. 3:8, 10

Paul kept seeking knowledge of God all the way to the end of his life. Seeking to know God more pleases him. That is what he said through the prophet Jeremiah.

Thus says the LORD: "Let not the wise man boast in his wisdom, let not the mighty man boast in his might, let not the rich man boast in his riches, but let him who boasts boast in this, that he understands and knows me, that I am the LORD who practices steadfast love, justice, and righteousness in the earth. For in these things I delight, declares the LORD."
—Jer. 9:23–24

On a mission trip in the Maasai Mara of Kenya, we learned from the Maasai warriors that they never leave the village to care for their flocks without their special lion club. It's a hardwood club about 20 inches long and only about an inch or two in diameter. On the end of the club is a knob about the size of a baseball that hangs off to one side. That knob has a tiny point on the side. This little tip is meant to be the point of contact with the lion's forehead. Many lions have been slain by this small club in a warrior's hand. Do you realize how close the Maasai would have to be to the lion in order to hit him in the head with a 20-inch club? Many warriors told us of such encounters with the lion within reach and ready to pounce. They actually waited until the lion was in midair and then swung that little yet deadly and effective club.

Sometimes, Satan, the prowling lion, leaps right at our faces with his lies and temptations to make us waiver and turn away from the truth. He wants us to believe that our God is not enough to see us through the trials of life. He wants us to feel abandoned. Get out that sword. Smack that lion in the face with the Word of God. Cinch up that belt of truth. Claim your righteousness that comes from Jesus's sacrifice for you. Stand firm in those shoes of peace that surpass understanding. Hold up your faith as a shield of protection, and put that salvation on your head as you remember God's victory over sin and death. Just show up, but show up in full armor to the battle that God has already won.

Chapter 7

Lessons from Bloody Knees

Regardless of the cause of our adversity or ugly days, God has a purpose. Life is not a reality show. In spite of how it may feel, our struggles are not for God's entertainment. God is building character into each of us. He is pouring his wisdom into us through experiences. Our current situation is not the end of the story. Knowledge and wisdom often come from experience. Sometimes, the experience is positive through a classroom, training, or enjoyable life experience. At other times, the experiences can be negative, possibly a result of our own or someone else's mistakes.

David learned about being a warrior and leading from years of shepherding and protecting sheep. He learned how to battle wild animals, which in turn taught him how to confront Goliath. As king, he led people well, relying on his experiences of leading sheep to water or pastures and away from danger.[1]

Likewise, Moses learned to lead during 40 years of exile from Egypt while caring for his father-in-law's sheep.[2] Forty years! We always hear that sheep are dumb, yet in the Bible we see that God used sheep to teach leadership skills to his called ones. Jesus also spoke of his followers as sheep.[3] What experiences will it take us as "dumb" sheep to learn the lessons God has for us, to become the effective men and women of God who are useful for his kingdom?

Children learn to walk by getting up after falling down. They learn to play catch by continuing to play after taking a ball on the chin, and they learn to ride a bike by trying again after the spills and skinned knees. Of this I have firsthand knowledge.

I was in first grade and ready for my first bicycle. I had learned to ride because the cute and generous girl next door let me take turns on her bike. Sometimes, though, I was left on the front porch watching all the other girls ride off together. There weren't enough bikes to go around. I didn't have one.

Christmas was coming. This was my chance. I asked Santa for a small Schwinn just like the one the little girl next door rode. It was just my size, and it was cute, compact, and blue, my favorite color. Not having an abundance of funds, my parents decided that they (Santa) should get me a little larger bike so it would last me for several years, and at that time, Huffy bikes were more affordable. They always did their best for us with a limited income.

Well, Christmas came. I was so excited that I was awake all night. Would my cute, compact Schwinn be there? Would Santa come through for me? My two brothers and I lay on the upstairs floor throughout the night, trying to listen through the air vent to hear any evidence of Santa's arrival. By that time, my wiser, older, nine-year-old brother knew the truth. I had my suspicions, but it was much more fun to believe.

When it was still quite dark outside, our parents finally gave the okay to our pleas to run downstairs and discover our new treasures and toys. We came charging down the stairs and raced to the tree. I stood in awe. There it was! "Santa" had left me a beautiful blue Schw . . . Wait! What? Huffy? Maybe he misunderstood. It *was* blue. That was good. But it wasn't cute and small like my neighbor's. It was larger and quite practical looking. Practical is *not* appealing to a six-year-old girl wanting to fit in with the neighbor-hood girls. Cute and small is good. Large and practical is just, well, practical.

I tried to ride that large, practical bike. I just couldn't do it. It was too hard to reach the pedals. The ground was painfully too far away, and I had the skinned knees to prove it. Several spills and a number of Band-Aids later, I found myself sitting on the front porch again, elbows on my bloody knees and chin in my hands, watching the neighborhood girls ride.

"Come ride with us," cute neighbor with cute bike yelled.

"I can't," I pouted. "My bike is too big."

Upon my pitiful pronouncement, said cute neighbor offered to let me ride said cute bike, proposing that she would ride my larger, practical Huffy. Well, off we all went throughout the neighborhood. I was thrilled. I was no longer left out. I was one of the girls. That is how we rolled for several weeks.

For some unknown reason, my cute neighbor one day determined that practical no longer suited her. She wanted to ride her own cute bike. I was once again left on the front porch, chin in hands. Enough! I did not want to be left out anymore. I had tasted the goodness of belonging, and I could not tolerate the loneliness of the porch any longer. I got myself up on that Huffy and fell. I got up on that Huffy again and fell. Again. Again. Again. But by the end of that afternoon, my bloody knees were peddling alongside all the other girls of my hood. Such a feeling! Me and my Huffy—we belonged.

Trials, failures, pain, ugly days, and bloody knees. They are all part of life.

Would we want to save our children from all heartache? Sometimes, we say yes, but the truth is that they wouldn't know about danger without bumps, bruises, and burns. They would not be able to make decisions without the opportunity to make tough choices. They would not have compassion if they had not experienced need. They would not value friendship without losing a friend.

In the same way, our Heavenly Father allows his children to experience trials, failures, pain, ugly days, and bloody knees. Remember James?

For you know that the testing of your faith produces steadfastness.
And let steadfastness have its full effect, that you may be perfect and complete, lacking in nothing.

—James 1:3–4

Look at David's reflection:

It is good for me that I was afflicted,
*   that I might learn your statutes.*
                              —Ps. 119:71

David is able to say this with conviction because of his experiences. He was afflicted as Saul pursued him. He was afflicted as a result of his own sin and the death of his son. He later was afflicted as he was pursued and fought against his own son who wanted to take the throne. David was plagued with much affliction, yet in hindsight, he was able to say that it was good.

Paul's reflections on his own suffering are enlightening as well. His life after meeting Jesus was one of persecutions. Once he began to share the message of Jesus as the expected Messiah, the Jews began plotting to kill Paul and even made several attempts. Along with Barnabas, Paul was thrown out of Antioch. But they dusted themselves off and went to Iconium where the same thing happened. They pressed on to the next town, Lystra. Some of the Jews from Antioch and Iconium followed them there. They dragged Paul out, stoned him, and left him for dead. Paul got up, went back into town, and left the next day for Derbe.[4] Astonishingly, he and Barnabas then returned to Lystra, Iconium, and

Antioch to encourage the believers. Here's what they told them:

It is necessary to go through many hardships to enter the kingdom of God.
                                        —Acts 14:22b CSB

Over the course of his ministry, Paul was beaten, stoned, shipwrecked, and imprisoned, but he would not be stopped. He knew the eternal value of suffering. He knew that he was learning to rely on God and was becoming stronger. Paul knew God was building character in him. God was making him strong and giving him endurance through the power of the indwelling Holy Spirit. Lives were being changed, and the church was strengthened as a result of Paul's sufferings.[5]

For the moment all discipline seems painful rather than pleasant, but later it yields the peaceful fruit of righteousness to those who have been trained by it.
                                        —Heb. 12:11

I vividly remember a particular Sunday morning in 1977. Bonnie was about 18 months old, officially toddler age and toddling around the kitchen in her Sunday dress.

I was baking a coffee cake to take and share with my Bible study class, and my little daughter was eagerly "helping" and, of course, multiplying the time and effort needed to accomplish the task. I was running late, as usual, and rushing to throw dirty dishes into the dishwasher. The oven timer went off, so I grabbed a hot pad, threw open the oven door, and pulled out the steaming coffee cake. I only turned my back for a split second, but in that time, Bonnie reached her little arm across the open oven door and laid it right down on that 350-degree door. My heart stopped at her scream. I dropped the coffee cake, snatched up my baby, and ran for the bathroom. Chuck met me halfway. I passed Bonnie to him as we ran together. I turned on the cold water full force while Chuck, holding her in his arms, jumped in the shower. Fully dressed in their Sunday best, he held Bonnie's little arm in that cold water to cool and soothe the burn.

I would never have wanted my daughter to experience a burn like that, and all these years later, I still hold myself responsible for her pain and suffering—one of many mom-fails through the years. However, Bonnie and I both learned some valuable lessons that day. She, of course, learned about the danger of hot ovens and consequential burns. I learned to *never* turn my back on a toddler when the oven door is open and, in fact, to never leave it open.

Fortunately for us, God doesn't make mistakes like leaving oven doors open, but he does allow the circumstances of our lives to teach us, grow us, and change us in order to conform us to the image of his Son. My daughters are grown up with children of their own now, but sometimes I look back and marvel at all God has done in their lives in spite of their parents' many mistakes and decisions.

If you would ask either of my daughters today, they would say they are thankful for the hardships they encountered in their early years. At the time, however, they probably would have given much different answers. Bonnie was 12 and Kelley was almost nine when we pulled them out of their church home, public school, and life as they knew it in California. Kelley was an up and comer in softball, and Bonnie was already an all-star. I had plenty of mommy guilt as we left the country to begin our missionary journey in Costa Rica. We were depriving our daughters of a "normal life" and all the extracurricular activities that went along with it. They could have been softball stars. Oh, we knew on a spiritual level we were obeying God's call, but on that human, protective, parent level, we were worried about the impact on our girls.

Their first hurdle was the language. It is hard for any child to start over in a new school and a new church in a new community, but when two young English speakers are suddenly immersed in Spanish, the transition is much more difficult. Worship and Sunday school were the hardest. Our first Sunday at our new church was an adventure. First, we walked about half a mile to the bus stop where we caught the Periferica into downtown San Jose, about a 20-minute ride. Then we walked another half mile to another bus stop where we caught the mini-bus (meenee boos) to Heredia, a small town about 30 minutes outside the city. Yes, we had to leave for church an hour and a half before worship started.

The girls found themselves in a Sunday school class where they did not understand a single word and worshiping in a service where some of the tunes were familiar, but the words were unrecognizable. By the time we made our hour-and-a-half trek back home, we were all dazed. If ever we needed an afternoon nap, that was the day.

Language acquisition for the girls was slow. They went to a British school where they had an hour of Spanish lessons each day, but that was not nearly enough to make them comfortable at church or even going to the little convenience store next to our house to buy a Fanta Naranja or a candy bar. We hired a tutor for them, but the girls were uncomfortable and shy with her. After about four weeks, the tutor quit, so we let that plan go.

When we eventually got to Spain to serve, the girls were suddenly motivated to speak the language and make friends in our church. They literally were fluent within weeks. The frustrations in Costa Rica had paid off. I was so jealous. The girls actually loved living in Spain. They found a community of youth who loved and accepted them from the beginning. It was a good fit for them, and they embraced the Spanish culture as their own. Their greater challenge came upon reentry into the United States.

We came back to the States in time for Bonnie to complete her senior year in public high school and for Kelley to begin ninth grade. They were back in school with a lot of the kids they had left five years before. There is a term that international workers use to describe their children: third-culture kids. The fact is that when you take a child from one culture and place them in a new culture, they partially connect with both cultures. Conversely, they partially disconnect with both cultures. They have become a blend of the two, and some consequently feel like outsiders in both.

Bonnie, the more social of the two, seemed to reenter the California world of high school pretty well, and later at Baylor, she found her niche with a group of other missionary kids (MKs) who were also multicultural. There is a special bond among MKs that is inexplicable yet tangible. They may have never met before, but once they know they share the MK life, they are knit together in spirit. It's a special thing.

Bonnie carried her multicultural experiences into her career as an educator. She has a compassion for her students that comes from experiences unique to being a third-culture kid. These insights have also made her an amazing mother who thinks outside the box and treats each of her four children as unique individuals. She has a heart for the Lord and for ministry in whatever opportunity God gives her.

Kelley had a harder go of it. To explain, let me retrace a little. The girls had been in public grade school in Vacaville, California, when we left for Costa Rica and language school. In Costa Rica, they attended a British private school. We then did a year of home schooling in anticipation of living in a remote area of Venezuela. That assignment never materialized, and the girls next found themselves in a school for missionary kids in Madrid, Spain. One year later we were on the island of Mallorca where the girls attended a private British school primarily for ambassadors' and embassy employees' kids. That year proved to be nonproductive, so we returned to home schooling for our third year in Spain. Then we returned to California where both girls attended the public Vacaville High

School. Bonnie went on to Baylor, but then we found ourselves in Texas where Kelley entered Grace Preparatory Academy while we waited for God to show us our next step. When we were called to Forest Cove Baptist Church in Kingwood, Texas, Kelley entered Kingwood High School as a sophomore midyear. This was Kelley's ninth school in eight years, and she will tell you that this one was the hardest transition of all.

Kelley had always been a very shy child, and all the school changes only accentuated this characteristic. On her first day at Kingwood High, she found herself in the universally dreaded situation of having lunch all by herself. She came home that afternoon and cried. I cried with her. The next day was the same, and so was each day after for the first two weeks. I wanted so very much to fix it, but I was powerless to do anything. All I could do was pray with her and for her.

Finally, she connected with one girl, Ellen, at church. Ellen had school lunch at the same hour. They agreed to meet. From that point on, Kelley had a small nucleus of friends, and with that she was content. If you ask Kelley today, she will tell you that as difficult as those transitions were, especially the last one, she is thankful that God prepared her for her future. It was during those difficult Kingwood days that God spoke to her heart and called her to overseas work. She has drawn upon those experiences to know that God is sufficient in all circumstances, even now as she serves in an undisclosed location with her husband and three children. Through all those school changes, God built into her the character that he knew she would need to fulfill his calling on her life. Both of our daughters today are women of character, faithfully serving as God leads them.

To the Romans (and to Bonnie, Kelley, you, and me), Paul wrote this:

> *Not only that, but we rejoice in our sufferings, knowing that suffering produces endurance, and endurance produces character, and character produces hope, and hope does not put us to shame, because God's love has been poured into our hearts through the Holy Spirit who has been given to us.*
>
> —Rom. 5:3–5

Chapter 8

But It's My Fault

Our suffering can be the result of many things, but sometimes, it comes from our own mistakes or the consequences of our sin. You may be thinking, "Yes, but how can I expect God to help me when this is my fault?" We all have made mistakes in life, some large and some small, and afterward, we've had to suffer the consequences of our actions or decisions. Sometimes there are solutions, but many times, we are left to deal with the hardships we have created for ourselves. Is there still joy to be found? Can God help us in those situations? Let me shout a resounding *yes*. He can, and he does if we only come to him with a repentant heart.

King Saul is an example of suffering as a result of his disobedience to God. Israel had clamored for God to give them a king to lead them just as all the other nations had—a king to lead them in battle. After many pleas by the people, God chose Saul to be King of Israel. The only condition was that Saul and the people of Israel had to follow all the commands of God. It was all going pretty well until, faced with yet another battle, Saul was waiting for Samuel to come and offer the pre-battle sacrifice. Eager to do battle and short on patience, Saul decided to go against God's laws and statutes by offering up the sacrifice on his own. Why not? He was quite capable of starting a fire. Why should he have to wait for God's prophet? Wasn't he the king, after all? Samuel finally arrived, saw the fire burning, and exclaimed, "What have you done?"[1]

Saul made his excuses. Look at his pathetic response.

When I saw that the people were scattering from me, and that you did not come within the days appointed, and that the Philistines had mustered at Michmash, I said, "Now the Philistines will come down against me at Gilgal, and I have not sought the favor of

the LORD." So I forced myself, and offered the
burnt offering.

—1 Sam. 13:11–12

"I forced myself." I forced myself to be disobedient
to God's law? Saul's excuses did not impress God or
Samuel.

And Samuel said to Saul, "You have done fool-
ishly. You have not kept the command of the
LORD your God, with which he commanded
you. For then the LORD would have established
your kingdom over Israel forever. But now
your kingdom shall not continue. The LORD
has sought out a man after his own heart, and
the LORD has commanded him to be prince
over his people, because you have not kept
what the LORD commanded you."

—1 Sam. 13:13–14

Saul's consequences were severe. He would soon
lose the very kingdom for which he went to battle. He
had tried to lead Israel with his own strength and wisdom. He had failed miserably. Sadly, even after this
hard lesson, Saul again disobeyed God's direct commands during the last days of his reign.[2]

What do we learn from Saul's sad story? Saul was too proud to admit he was wrong. He continually tried to justify his actions. He failed to recognize God's authority over his life. We must accept responsibility for our own actions. We must repent, turn to God, and let him give us the strength to face our consequences. It is so easy in our shame to turn away from God and look to other things and people for comfort. Samuel gave Saul and all the people of Israel sound advice.

> *If you will fear the LORD and serve him and obey his voice and not rebel against the commandment of the LORD, and if both you and the king who reigns over you will follow the LORD your God, it will be well. But if you will not obey the voice of the LORD, but rebel against the commandment of the LORD, then the hand of the LORD will be against you and your king . . . And Samuel said to the people, "Do not be afraid; you have done all this evil. Yet do not turn aside from following the LORD, but serve the LORD with all your heart. And do not turn aside after empty things that cannot profit or deliver, for they are empty."*
> —1 Sam. 12:14–15, 20–21

Unfortunately, Saul and the people of Israel did not follow Samuel's wise counsel. Sadly, we also fail to heed these wise words. We turn to our own reasoning or to the norms of our society that tell us our actions are fine, acceptable, and normal. God's standards are clear. Don't turn to the empty things of the world, but rather turn to God with a repentant heart. Allow him to do what the world and our society cannot. He will restore you, refresh you, and make you whole.

David, Saul's successor, also made some grave errors in judgment. After being king of Israel for several years and after years of listening to God and obeying, David seemed to become complacent. In the spring when kings march out to war, David didn't. Instead of seeking God's direction and leading his men in battle, David stayed home gazing out the window.[3]

I must interject that I do not sit in judgment of David. I will not cast the first stone. How often do I get tired of engaging in the battle of life's challenges? Sometimes, I just want to stay home in bed. Some days, gazing out the window sounds pretty good. In fact, sometimes we need that break from the battlefield, and God knows that. He is gracious, understanding, and compassionate. He understands rest. Jesus even took time out from ministry to rest and pray. Several times we read in the Gospels that he separated himself from the crowds and at times from the disciples as well.[4]

Unfortunately, David was not using his rest time to seek God. In fact, he sought out the company of Bathsheba instead. As he gazed out the window, he saw this beautiful woman bathing on the roof of her house down the hill from the palace.[5] David had a choice to make. He could either turn to God and put what he had seen out of his mind, or he could act upon his fleshly impulses. Again, I find it difficult to cast stones. Whether it is a decision to act upon a lustful, sexual impulse, to lie to get out of a tight spot, or to gluttonously eat six freshly baked cookies, we all "have sinned and fall short of the glory of God" (Rom. 3:23). We also pay the consequences for our actions.

Bathsheba conceived a son due to their encounter, leading David into sin upon sin. In trying to cover up his indiscretion, he essentially murdered Bathsheba's husband, Uriah, by putting him on the front lines of battle.[6] David thought he had successfully gotten away with murder, but Nathan, the prophet, came to David with a word from the Lord.

Thus says the LORD, "Behold, I will raise up evil against you out of your own house. And I will take your wives before your eyes and give them to your neighbor, and he shall lie with your wives in the sight of this sun. For you did it secretly, but I will do this thing before all Israel and before the sun." David said to Nathan, "I have sinned against the LORD." And Nathan said to David, "The LORD also has put away your sin; you shall not die. Nevertheless, because by this deed you have utterly scorned the LORD, the child who is born to you shall die."

—2 Sam. 12:11–14

Forgiveness from God does not mean we are free from the consequences of our actions. David paid dearly for his affair with Bathsheba and the murder of Uriah. The baby Bathsheba gave birth to became deathly ill. David fasted and prayed in repentance, but God's judgment had been pronounced. The baby died.[7] David's family suffered many more tragedies in the years to come due to God's judgment. Later, one of David's other sons would pursue him and try to murder him as he sought to take his father's throne.[8]

Sin tears families apart. Children reject parents. Parents reject children. Siblings reject each other. Husbands and wives divorce. It is only through forgiveness and the grace of God that healing can take place, yet many times relationships are never restored. Sometimes, a death prevents reconciliation. Sometimes, forgiveness is elusive or one-sided. God will still give grace to your broken heart. Whatever the sin, God not only forgives a repentant heart but also gives grace to endure or even overcome the consequence. Do not discount his pardon. Embrace his mercy.

In the fall, when young high school graduates go off to college to study, I didn't. Oh, I went off to college all right, but the study part was definitely neglected. Chuck and I, being the mature 18-year-olds that we were, decided to go to the same college. We often tell the story that we majored in each other. We spent way too much time together and way too little time doing homework assignments or studying. We found the party scene on campus as well. The beer and wine flowed, and this good Christian girl found herself imbibing and often drunk. Enjoying the freedom of no adult supervision, Chuck and I found ourselves becoming more and more intimate. We knew it was wrong, but we allowed temptation to overtake us.

This is not a story I am proud of, and until this writing, I have not told it publicly. After weeks of indulging our fleshly desires and just before Christmas break, I realized my period was late. I was frantic with worry, and thoughts of all the consequences of my actions flooded my mind. I shared the terrifying news with Chuck. He was visibly shaken with the realization that he may have fathered a child. Not being 100 percent sure, we agreed to wait it out a few more days. We went home to our respective families for Christmas. I was a sulking, moody college student. For me, this Christmas break was not the joyful family gathering and celebration of the past. It was the building tension of knowing I had to face the truth, *and* I had to talk to my parents.

Back in December 1970, only the so-called bad girls got pregnant. At least that's what I thought. How had this good Christian girl, the daughter of a church deacon and a deaconess, the daughter of youth group directors, the daughter of my spiritual idols, fallen so low? How had she committed so great a sin? I was broken, and I thought I was hopeless. I didn't know how to tell my parents. I waited. I fretted. I cried. One afternoon, I was lying across my mom's bed watching her wrap Christmas presents.

"I am having a Christmas party for the high school girls this weekend," Mom said. "I was hoping maybe you would share a testimony for them as the devotional."

My heart sank. There was a huge pit in my gut, and I knew the dreaded moment had come. I was about to vomit.

"I don't think I can do that, Mom."

"You can't?"

"Um, no. I haven't really been living like I should at college. I don't think I have a good testimony to share. I've been drinking a lot for one thing."

She waited.

"Well, I might as well tell you. You're going to find out eventually anyway." Tears started to flow.

"You're pregnant." She calmly stated.

"Yes. How did you know?" I wailed.

"I suspected."

She then asked all the appropriate questions without condemnation, yet I could feel her disappointment. How late was I? Had I been to a doctor for confirmation? Had Chuck and I talked about it? Did we have a plan?

A plan? The pit grew bigger at the thought of a baby. At that time, the concept of single parenting was one of an abandoned, rejected soul with a child—an outcast. Then there was the thought of marriage. Chuck and I had struggled while dating to understand each other since we came from two very distinct backgrounds. Adding a baby to a new marriage sounded like certain divorce before the "I dos" could even be pronounced. Abortion—it had just been voted legal in the state of Washington, effective January 1971.

For a girl who always thought abortion was wrong, now facing the humiliation of her parents before the church and the daunting image of motherhood, abortion suddenly didn't seem so bad. However, I believed that either way, I was going to lose Chuck. Keep the baby—disaster. Abortion—gone our separate ways forever. Adoption—I couldn't even grasp the concept. I was 18 and felt like my life was over. I had messed up, failed my parents, and failed God. I wanted to die.

Chuck and I talked a few times over break, but we avoided the obvious. It was too hard to talk about it. Finally, back at school, we had "the discussion." Neither one of us felt ready for parenthood, yet Chuck did offer to marry me. It felt like a "have to" rather than a "want to." In reality, I guess it was. I didn't want to marry someone out of a "have to." Chuck didn't want me to raise his baby without him. Abortion was wrong. That's what I had always believed. I was facing the reality that no matter what we did, our relationship would be over. I didn't see how it could withstand all these obstacles.

Then one of us said it. I don't even remember which one of us proposed the idea. "What if we got married *and* had the abortion?" We would be able to start a marriage fresh, making a firm commitment to each other without the added intensity of trying to raise a child. While knowing it was not a great decision, to this terrified 18-year-old, it sounded like a solution that gave us the best shot at a future together. Notice that there was no prayer involved in this decision, just the selfish, misguided wisdom of two teenagers.

We called our parents and told them what we had decided. We scheduled the now legal abortion for the following week and planned a wedding in two weeks' time. There were rumors because of the quick wedding, of course, but no baby ever came, and few people ever knew the truth.

Consequences? Oh, there have been many. They didn't surface at first, but there was always the sense within me, the knowledge, that what I had done was wrong. It made me sad sometimes. It wasn't until I had a miscarriage that I really came to grips with what I had done. When Bonnie, our oldest, was about 18 months old, I lost a baby at only 10 weeks. Naturally, I was devastated, but the awful realization came that I was grieving for this baby because it was wanted, planned for, and loved.

The reality came crashing down on me as I wept uncontrollably for my first baby—the one I had killed— only because he was not wanted. The grief came in waves after that. I began to try to make amends the only way I knew how. I asked God for forgiveness. I asked Chuck for forgiveness. He in turn asked me for forgiveness. We asked my parents for forgiveness. They wept with us and asked for forgiveness for not trying to talk us out of our decision. We all grieved together. That grief will always be with me. The tears flow even now as I write. Regret is such a small, insignificant word that doesn't even come close to the feelings that still remain.

There have been a few times over the years when I have had the opportunity to counsel women who are grieving after an abortion. I have been able to confidentially share my story with them, grieve with them, and assure them of God's merciful forgiveness and grace. God's grace—it is a gift that we receive and also give to others.

Christmas break, 27 years later, we would give that grace. It was a Saturday.

"Mom." Bonnie and I were riding in the car. "I have to tell you something," her voice quavered.

I knew. I suddenly knew that calm my mother had demonstrated 27 years before. I felt and gave that amazing grace.

"I think I'm pregnant," she wept. I pulled the car into a parking lot, turned off the engine, and reached out to hold my precious daughter. I asked all the pertinent questions, just as my mom had done. But then I told her my story. I told her about grace. We prayed together. Then we went to buy a pregnancy test. I can still vividly remember the scene, the two of us huddled in the grocery store bathroom anxiously awaiting the results. It confirmed her fears, so we headed home together to face her dad.

We walked in the door of the house, and apparently Chuck was about to leave. He was standing in the entry-way as we came in.

"What's wrong?" He could tell immediately that something was off.

"Bonnie has something she needs to tell you," I said. He looked at his daughter.

"Dad, I'm so sorry to disappoint you this way and bring shame on you as a pastor," she said as she fought back the tears. "I'm pregnant."

Chuck was totally taken off guard. His agitation grew as he began to ask questions. "When?" "How?" "Who is this guy?" "How could you?"

"Wait! Wait!" I said. "She is just like you and me, so be careful what you say."

He looked at me, looked at Bonnie, and said, "I'll be back later." Then he walked out the door.

"What do I do, Mom? What can I say to him?" Bonnie was crying again.

"I don't know, Baby. You just need to pray for wisdom and the right words. Give him some time." She went up to her room, cried, and prayed.

I prayed, too, and I waited. Several hours later, Chuck came home.

"I just needed to think," he told me, as the two of us stood in the kitchen quietly talking. "I needed to process my feelings without hurting anyone. In reality, there is nothing I want more than to wrap my arms around her and tell her all is forgiven and everything will be okay. But I need her to be repentant—not just sorry she got pregnant, but repentant for all that got her into this situation. I need to mirror the love and forgiveness of the Heavenly Father. That's my heart. I just need to hear the right words from her."

Bonnie stayed in her room the rest of the day, and the tension in our home was palpable. The next day, Sunday, Chuck was actually on vacation, so we were able to go to worship together as a family. We filed into the back row of the worship center, and as God ordained it, Bonnie ended up sitting between Chuck and me. I can't really remember what the message was about other than it dealt with restoration and forgiveness. Our little row of family was somewhat weepy during the service, and then during the invitation song, the miracle happened. Bonnie leaned over and began to whisper in her daddy's ear. Soon his arms were wrapped around her as they wept together.

Later that afternoon, I walked into the living room to find Chuck and Bonnie across from each other sitting cross-legged on the sofa, hands entwined.

"Now you need to take care of yourself and that baby, you understand?"

Later that same afternoon, Chuck and Frank, Bonnie's boyfriend, took a long drive together. They talked about accountability, repentance, and forgiveness. I'm sure it's one of the hardest conversations Frank has ever had, but it laid the foundation for an open and loving relationship with our future son-in-law.

Unbeknownst to Bonnie, Frank had already bought a ring. Even before knowing the results of the pregnancy test, Frank had already made up his mind. He wanted Bonnie to be his wife. He wanted to establish a God-honoring relationship with the girl he loved. By the end of the day, Bonnie had a restored relationship with her dad and was engaged to the father of her child. She was about to begin her semester of student teaching, and in her words, she did not want to be a "bad example" to her students by being single and pregnant. Bonnie, Frank, Chuck, and I looked at the calendar. Knowing we needed a little time to prepare but honoring Bonnie's desire to not wait long, we looked at the end of January. As it turned out, January 30th was available, which just so happened to be the same date Chuck and I had gotten married. It seemed like a little wink from God.

Monday morning, I went to work, and Chuck went to the church intending to talk immediately with our senior pastor. We wanted to be up front with everyone about our family's situation and our intentions moving forward. About 9:00 a.m., I received a phone call from our pastor. Hearing his voice, I was apprehensive, not knowing what to expect.

"Karen, this is your pastor. I just had a long conversation with Chuck, and I just want you to know that your family has my full support and the support of this church. We will do whatever we can to walk with you through this journey. I don't want you to ever feel that you cannot hold your head high when you walk into this building. You, Bonnie, and your entire family are loved and will be lifted up in any way we can."

Wow! I'm not sure what I expected from my pastor, but it wasn't a loving phone call of encouragement and support. His wife also called me and offered to set up a meeting with me, Bonnie, and some other ladies of the church to help us pull off a wedding in less than 30 days. Our church family rallied around us as if Bonnie were their own daughter. One deacon's wife took me shopping for a mother-of-the-bride dress. Another took me to buy shoes and a bag. A florist in the church offered flowers at no cost, and the rest of the decorations were made and donated by other precious women. All the food for the reception was donated by church members, and the spread looked like a professionally catered feast. The only things we paid for throughout the planning and wedding were Bonnie's dress, Chuck's tuxedo, Kelley's maid of honor dress, and the cake. That is all. That is grace. Our church family gave us the gift of a wedding for our daughter. They gave us the gift of grace.

How different Bonnie's experience was from my own. She chose repentance and received grace. I, like David, had chosen sin upon sin. Grace was long in coming for me as I endured my grief.

Grace and forgiveness? Yes! Consequences? Absolutely! Bonnie and Frank also had consequences. They suddenly had to find a place to live, provide for themselves and a baby, and finish college. They found a little two-bedroom rental house in an older neighborhood of Waco, Texas, a yet unfound fixer upper that would not be fixed up. It had no air conditioning, minimal heating, and a tiny kitchen. The back door oddly entered through the second bedroom that would become the nursery. Bonnie and Frank continued to work, attend classes, and prepare for their child on their tight budget. It was a hard road, but God gave them grace.

A word must be said about the baby. That little boy, Michael, was such a gift from the Lord! He was the ultimate healing for all of us. He was the final salve to all the wounds. God has a special plan for that boy who is now a young man with a wife of his own.

Both Michael and Callie, his precious bride, have a heart for the Lord and for seeing others come to know him. They are active in ministry and diligent to follow God's ideals.

I will always grieve for the child that should have been, but I am so thankful for this grandson of mine who will always be a reminder of *grace*.

Shame is a hard thing to process and a very difficult, self-inflicted trial to endure. Shame is the result of hidden sin. Shame makes us want to hide our past mistakes. It makes us feel like the person we project ourselves to be is fake. People don't know who we really are. If they really knew, they would reject us. It makes us feel like we don't deserve the love of family, friends, or fellow believers. It's hard to see the joy in that. I suppose the writing of this chapter is, in some way, a release of my own shame, yet I was reminded many years ago that Jesus not only took all my sin on the cross, but he also bore my shame. The shame that I deserve rests on his shoulders. Part of accepting the gift of salvation is the vindication from all our sin as well as the shame that accompanies it. Therein is the joy.

Shame is what the prodigal son felt when he planned to go home and ask for a demotion, from son to servant.

I will arise and go to my father, and I will say to him, "Father, I have sinned against heaven and before you. I am no longer worthy to be called your son. Treat me as one of your hired servants."

—Luke 15:18–19

His father would have no part in such a demotion.[9] Just like our Heavenly Father, his only desire was to celebrate and rejoice over his son's return and repentance. God does not demote us because of our mistakes. All he asks is that we repent and allow him to rejoice over us.

I don't know what your past holds, my friend, but I can assure you that God does not want you to reside in your shame. If you have chosen repentance, then you can rest not only in his forgiveness but also in his release of your shame. Let it go! Abide in his *grace* and his *joy*. Join the celebration.

Chapter 9

But It Hurts!
When God's People Are Ungodly

There are times when we suffer just because vindictive people want to hurt us. Paul most definitely encountered hateful opposition from the very ones who had been his colleagues. They hated him. They hated his new faith in Jesus. Everywhere he went, the devout Jews sought to beat him, stone him, or imprison him.[1] Some so-called believers even sought to compete rather than collaborate. But look what Paul says about it from prison.

Some indeed preach Christ from envy and rivalry, but others from good will. The latter do it out of love, knowing that I am put here for the defense of the gospel. The former proclaim Christ out of selfish ambition, not sincerely but thinking to afflict me in my imprisonment. What then? Only that in every way, whether in pretense or in truth, Christ is proclaimed, and in that I rejoice. Yes, and I will rejoice.

—Phil. 1:15–18

Paul saw the greater purpose. His focus was not on himself or his circumstances. His eyes were fixed on Jesus and the message of redemption for all human-kind. Paul was passionate about getting that message out. He wasn't about to get side-tracked with periph-eral issues or concerns over his physical comfort. He knew his circumstances were the result of obedience to Christ. In that, he took pleasure.

Paul's suffering was not his fault. He was doing exactly what God had called him to do, yet many for-mer friends didn't like it. Paul understood that not everyone would embrace the message of Christ. He understood that some would superimpose their own grief, hurt, strife, or envy on the gospel message and try to distort the truth either for their own advantage or simply to do damage to Paul. His only concern was that the truth be proclaimed, and in that he rejoiced. God's calling is an honor and privilege, but with that calling come challenges and sometimes pain.

After several years of ministry and a few years on the mission field, I thought I had been through enough dark days for one lifetime, yet I was soon to encounter a period of complete and utter darkness that impacted my husband even more than me. Chuck was serving as missions pastor of a fairly large Texas church as well as serving as one of the four executive staff who led alongside the senior pastor.

Discontent began to emerge from the congregation with regard to the senior pastor. Most of the discontent stemmed from the pastor's personality, preaching style, and leadership style, although some were taking issue with his theology and made accusations of egocentricity. Since none of the charges were for immoral conduct or for any illegal issue, the executive staff believed that according to scripture and wise counsel sought from other respected and godly men, God's called and anointed leader should not be forcibly removed. They agreed that God should be the only one to remove the pastor from the role to which God had called him. They pressed forward, honoring and respecting the office of senior pastor.

As the weeks and months passed, the tension in the congregation grew until the deacons, many of whom were discontented, called a special meeting with the senior pastor and the executive staff. They presented the senior pastor with charges and accusations, to which he vigorously defended himself and refused to resign. The tensions continued to grow, and the entire staff was put under extreme pressure from all sides. Finally, after many months of dispute and dissension, the senior pastor called Chuck.

"I've decided to resign," he said.

"Okay," Chuck responded, not trying to talk him out of it but believing that God was, in fact, moving the senior pastor out.

The next day, a group of ardent senior pastor supporters called a meeting. They talked the senior pastor into withdrawing his resignation and called for a vote of confidence from the congregation. They believed that the discontented members were few but vocal and that the silent majority favored the senior pastor. It was a messy, ugly time in our church, pitting longtime friends against each other in unkind arguments, resulting in many severed relationships.

The vote date was set, and the private ballots were cast. Fortunately, Chuck and I had to be away at a conference that weekend and did not have to vote. It did not go well for the senior pastor, and he did finally resign.

Instead of alleviating the stress placed upon the four executive staff pastors, the resignation caused the tension to grow. Those who had opposed the senior pastor were angry with the executive staff, questioning why they had not helped remove the senior pastor sooner. Those who had supported the senior pastor were also angry with the executive staff, challenging them that they should have fought on his behalf to keep him there. Arguments among members were common, and attendance began to drop.

The executive staff then had the enormous responsibility and challenge to keep the church together until a new senior pastor could be found. It would have been very easy for any one of the four to move to a new position in a different church. They were physically, mentally, emotionally, and spiritually exhausted. The four men came together, prayed together, and covenanted together to stay. Their heart was to fight to protect God's church and see it through this crisis. They divvied up responsibilities and pressed on.

The battle was long. As attendance continued to diminish, one of the pressing issues became the budget. Expenses had *not* diminished, but the giving had dropped dramatically in direct parallel with the declining attendance. Bills had to be paid, and difficult decisions had to be made. Some of the staff had to be let go. The landscaping company had to be let go. Church members had to volunteer to care for flower beds and mow the lawns. Hours the facilities were available for activities were cut back in order to save on utilities. The executive staff even gave themselves a 20 percent salary cut.

Resources for virtually every ministry were reduced, and a new church budget was made. According to the by-laws, this new budget needed congregational approval, so a church business meeting was called. All the anger and frustration held in for months came firing out in all directions at the meeting. The staff was under a surprise attack and had not worn their armor. The verbal gunfire hit each one in their most vulnerable spots. It became apparent that the discussion was not about the budget but had become an opportunity for people to air their bottled-up feelings that had been suppressed during months of strain. They were no longer trusting anyone to handle church business, and they were loaded for bear. The silent majority was silent no longer.

After the meeting, the four executive staff members determined that it would be good to give the congregation an ongoing forum to express themselves, ask questions, and receive appropriate responses. A special e-mail address was set up for this purpose. That way, the church members could type out their anger and frustrations (or encouragement), and the staff was protected by the distance and wonder of the World Wide Web. In relegating responsibilities, the four decided that Chuck would receive all the e-mails. He was to read each one, determine whether it required an answer, and pass it on to the appropriate staff person for a response. If no response was required, the e-mail was discarded.

The venom my husband had to digest over the next few months nearly destroyed him. Many times, rather than share the nastiness of the e-mails with the other pastors, he read them, evaluated them, and deleted them. After all the months of negativity before the senior pastor resigned and now months of contentious e-mails, budget struggles, and heart-wrenching decisions, Chuck was empty. Throughout those many months, I often came home from work to find him on the living room sofa, curled up in a fetal position. He had stopped functioning. He gave everything he had at the office, fighting for the struggling church. When he came home each evening, he had nothing left.

My journey through those three years of strife was that of a wife agonizing for her husband and a church member heartbroken for her church. I struggled with resentment toward people I had loved dearly. I cried from pain, discouragement, and concern for Chuck's mental health. I worried since there was no relief in sight. I've often heard it said that hurt people hurt people. Well, our people were hurting, and in turn, they were hurting each other and our staff. It was a tragic period in the life of our church.

So where was the joy in that struggle? Where was my light in the darkness? Where was my *warm place in the sun*? It was in worship. I was part of the praise team at that time, and each week as I rehearsed, I would dwell on the truths of the lyrics. Each song seemed to have a message just for me. As we led worship, I would let God's reassuring love wash over me as the tears flowed. It was in those moments that I was reminded that God is faithful. God is great. God is good. He loves me. He sings over me. There is nothing too difficult for him. Praise pleases God, but it also ministers to us. As we proclaim the greatness of our God, we take the focus off ourselves and look at him. Then we are able to see him, not just in our worship but in our circumstances. I couldn't even open my Bible during that blackest time of our lives, but his Word penetrated my heart through music and lyrics of truth. God communicated with me through those songs, and he sustained me.

Is your pain unbearable? Worship! Is your hurt so deep that you don't know how to pray anymore? Praise

God! Regardless of your circumstances, God is faithful. He will never abandon you. He will never leave you defenseless.

I remember hearing the story from a friend of a couple who had struggled through the path and pain of infertility. After years of trying to conceive, they finally opted to adopt. They walked the long journey, followed all the steps, and jumped through all the hoops to finally qualify as adoptive parents. Then the waiting began until the long-anticipated phone call finally came. "We have a baby for you." Weeks later, the birth mother changed her mind. The couple was naturally heartbroken. Again, they waited for a phone call. Once again, a mother changed her mind. Finally, the third phone call came, and the baby was to be theirs. This time the mother would not change her mind. This time, the baby was in surgery with a serious heart condition. After weeks of fighting for his life, with the adoptive parents vigilantly praying by his side, the little baby boy passed away. I will never forget the words of the adoptive mother. She said, "I have changed so much of what I believe about God through this process. I have questioned him continually and have received no answers. The only thing I know for certain is that God is God."

God is God. Do you know how profound that is? That is praise in its simplest form. God. In just one word, we have deity, sovereignty, supremacy, the one we worship. Just to call him God is to worship. Knowing he is God is what we hang onto when we have nothing else. In reality, he is all we need.

> The LORD is my shepherd; I shall not want.
>   He makes me lie down in green pastures.
> He leads me beside still waters.
>   He restores my soul.
> He leads me in paths of righteousness
>   for his name's sake.
>
> Even though I walk through the valley of the shadow of death,
>   I will fear no evil, for you are with me;
>   your rod and your staff, they comfort me.
>
> You prepare a table before me
>   in the presence of my enemies;
> you anoint my head with oil; my cup overflows.
> Surely goodness and mercy shall follow me
>   all the days of my life,
> and I shall dwell in the house of the LORD
>   forever.

—Ps. 23:1–6

How often have we read or even quoted that passage, but do we really grasp the significance of what David is saying? David had been a shepherd for several years before becoming king of Israel.[2] He knew the role. He understood the relationship between the shepherd and his sheep. David knew how dependent sheep are. They need a shepherd. They won't survive without that shepherd looking after them. We can't survive the lions, wolves, and bears of this life that are waiting to attack us. We need Jesus, our Shepherd.

Our Shepherd provides for us. Our Shepherd gives us rest and restoration. He even teaches us to walk in obedience to him "for his name's sake." Remember that God's reputation is on the line as you traverse the path before you. He guides us in order to help us but also for the sake of his good name. He not only proves himself faithful to you personally but also to others who observe your faith. You can trust him because of his reputation. Others will trust him as they perpetuate that reputation with their faith.

The valley of the shadow of death may accurately describe your journey today. It certainly describes what Chuck and I experienced. This psalm exhorts us to not be afraid. In the Bible we read the words "fear not" or some form of "do not be afraid" over and over. Fear is the enemy, and God addresses it throughout scripture to Isaiah, to Mary, and to Joseph—to so many of the most faithful.[3] The list is long, but the reason is always the same: "I am with you." Whatever you are going through, God is with you, my friend, and worship will make you more aware of him.

The Shepherd also brings comfort with his presence. The rod and staff were the shepherd's tools to guide the sheep and protect them from predators. There are so many circumstances of life preying on our faith, yet God has the tools to protect us and guide us. Knowing that brings comfort. Even when I can't find my way through the darkness, I know that God will guide me and comfort me. Not only will he comfort me, but he will pamper me with his goodness. Yes, there is much to worship and praise God for, no matter your circumstances—just because he is God.

Have you been persecuted, slandered, or even abused through no fault of your own? Is your boss unbearable or your spouse just plain mean? Are you the victim of bullying and abuse? Have you suffered a rejection that still eats away at your self-worth? Oh, friend, turn to Jesus. He wants to comfort you. He wants to give you the grace and strength you need to bear each moment of your situation. Let him meet you in the darkness with his warm, comforting light. Not only will he sustain you but he will reveal himself to others through your endurance and faith.

What about my sweet husband? You may be wondering how he got through this darkest of trials. God gave Chuck strength and encouragement through the other executive staff. Those four men who prayed together and fought side by side formed a bond like no other. Someone during the course of the battle nicknamed them the Four Horsemen of the Apocalypse—the four who fought for the kingdom. Fred Dallas, Mark Terry, Barry Wilson, and Chuck Oak will always be knit together as only fellow warriors can be. In 2008, long after the battle, Chuck was called by God to another ministry. God called Fred home in 2018, but Mark and Barry still enjoy ministry at that same church they fought for so many years ago.

Chapter 10

That's Life

None of us want to be like Job. He lost everything—his possessions, his family, and even his own health, all for no apparent benefit to anyone. In the first wave of destruction, he lost his livestock, his servants, and his children.[1] Job's response is not at all what we would expect.

> *Then Job arose and tore his robe and shaved his head and fell on the ground and worshiped. And he said, "Naked I came from my mother's womb, and naked shall I return. The*

LORD gave, and the LORD has taken away; blessed be the name of the LORD."

In all this Job did not sin or charge God with wrong.

—Job 1:20–22

The second wave of suffering came in the form of boils from his head to his toes. As Job sat in his pain, even his wife told him to curse God and die. As his suffering continued, at times his faith waned. Surrounded by his friends—who I must say were not encouragers—Job questioned God. How could he allow such suffering to one so faithful?[2] God's response puts all of us in our place.

Where were you when I laid the foundation of the earth?
   Tell me, if you have understanding.
Who determined its measurements—surely you know!
   Or who stretched the line upon it?
On what were its bases sunk,
   or who laid its cornerstone,
when the morning stars sang together
   and all the sons of God shouted for joy? . . .

Have you commanded the morning since your days began,

    and caused the dawn to know its place?

                —Job 38:4–7, 12

How dare we question God? Diseases, illnesses, even mosquito bites happen because sin entered the world when Adam and Eve disobeyed God.[3] We all have disobeyed God,[4] so we really can't blame Adam and Eve for all our maladies, but our illnesses are not usually a direct result of a specific sin in our lives, either.

In November 2007, I was diagnosed with breast cancer. I do not believe God was punishing me for any of the wrongs I had committed in my life, but I definitely suffered the effects of a sinful world.

They said I had dense, fibrocystic breasts, so for many years I suffered the indignity of biannual mammograms, always immediately followed by an ultrasound to look more closely at the dense tissue. The procedures, while painful and a bit humiliating, became routine for me, but that November day was different. Instead of going my merry way after the ultrasound, the technician asked me to wait to speak to the radiologist. "Well, that's odd," I thought to myself.

The day had already been unusual. Normally, Chuck went with me to the Medical Center for my appointments. We lived in Kingwood, Texas, at the time, about 30 minutes from the Houston Medical Center. We used our doctors' appointments as an opportunity to spend time together, grab lunch, and just hang out. On this particular day, Chuck had a meeting he could not miss, so I set out for the Medical Center on my own. No big deal until I realized that I was almost out of gas and had forgotten to bring cash and had no credit cards with me. Not good. When I realized my predicament, I called Chuck to talk through my options. We agreed that I should go to my appointment and then go to the bank conveniently located in the same building and cash a check. Problem solved.

The radiologist came to get me, escorted me to her office, and asked me to sit down. My foreboding grew. She took a seat next to me and began to explain that in my last mammogram six months before, they had noticed some calcifications in my milk ducts. It had been simply noted in my chart to follow the progress. The issue now was that the calcifications had increased, and the radiologist recommended needle biopsies in both breasts—two places in the right and one location in the left. We agreed that I should go forward with the biopsies right then. I was eager for answers, and they had an opening. I called Chuck to let him know what was happening because I knew my delay would cause him to think I had run out of gas.

Chuck could hear in my voice that I was a bit shaken. "Do you want me to come down there?" he asked. "I can ride my motorcycle down." Knowing he didn't like to ride in the city and thinking of his schedule, I assured him that I would be fine. I would go to the bank after the biopsies, get some gas, and head for home. Piece of cake.

At that point, I must admit that had I known what the needle biopsy involved, I would have waited and steeled myself for the event. I was not prepared to be strapped on a tall table, breasts exposed, and then be flipped over so the technicians below could easily access my upper body while the scanner guided them to the questionable calcifications. Nor was I prepared for the pain of that very large needle going in and grabbing a chunk of my breasts—three times!

After this somewhat stressful experience and with throbbing breasts, I dressed and proceeded to the bank for my cash. I wanted that gas so I could get home and process my trauma and the fact that I may have cancer. I needed a hug from my husband. While I was waiting in line for the teller, I got a text from Chuck.

"Where are you?"

Assuming that he thought I should be on my way home, I answered, "Just finished biopsies."

"Where are you?" he texted again.

"Still at the Medical Center."

"Where *are* you?"

"In the bank." I couldn't figure out what his issue was with my location.

With shaky hands, I wrote my check and received my cash. I turned to leave, and there entering the bank was my considerate, compassionate, and concerned husband. I let his arms wrap around me, and the pent-up tears flowed. Oh, it's good to feel loved! We spent an hour or so in a nearby coffee shop where I was able to talk and release my distress. He offered to leave his motorcycle in the parking garage and drive me home, but I assured him I was, by this time, sufficiently calm to drive. We caravanned to a gas station and then home.

A week later as we were pulling in the driveway, I got the phone call. We sat there in the car, Chuck in the driver's seat watching me closely and holding my hand as I spoke with a different radiologist.

"DCIS," he said. "Ductal carcinoma in situ. Not even stage one."

"So it's pre-cancer?" I asked.

"Oh no, it's definitely cancer. We just caught it very early." I was still. I listened. "We have scheduled you for an MRI. Get that done, and then talk to your GYN. You will also need to select a surgeon."

I was calm. Looking back, there are only two explanations I can come up with. One, I expected the diagnosis to be cancer since I had dealt with my problematic breasts for years. This was no surprise. Why should I be exempt from a disease that impacts so many women? And two, I could feel God's presence and peace. I was calm.

The journey had begun. After the MRI, I received a call from my GYN. "I'm looking at your report here. It looks like you have DCIS in your right breast, a suspicious area in your left, and the MRI shows . . . Oh my, you have a lot going on here. You need to contact a surgeon right away."

"What about an oncologist?" I asked.

"No, you just need to call a surgeon."

This is where Second Baptist Church of Houston rises to the top. Chuck and I were both on staff at the church's North Campus in Kingwood, Texas. Chuck was the Evangelism and New Members Pastor, and I was the Worship and Special Events Coordinator. The first day in the office after receiving my diagnosis, I went into the office of my supervisor, Mark Terry. He saw the look in my eyes and immediately dismissed everyone else from his office. He knew. He enveloped me in a big brotherly hug and prayed for me. We then invited the rest of our worship staff into the office to share the news with them. Love. I was surrounded by love, support, and encouragement.

How do you choose a surgeon in a city filled with surgeons? I had no idea where to begin. "Call John Barksdale," someone told me. "He is connected with the Medical Center. He will know who to recommend." John Barksdale worked at the church's main campus in the Pastoral Care Department. I called John.

"Let me make some phone calls," he said.

The next day, John had names and phone numbers for me.

"But which one do I call?" I asked him.

"Well, my friend, who is a plastic surgeon, said that if it were his wife, he would want Dr. Mike Coselli to be her surgeon."

I called Dr. Coselli's office and got an appointment for the following week. They tell you (whoever "they" are) that you should not be in a hurry to make decisions when you get a cancer diagnosis. But I can assure you of this: Once you know you have cancer, you want it *out*. You want it out ASAP. By this time, it was the beginning of December. Christmas was coming, my favorite time of the year, and I wanted—I *needed* some resolution.

Chuck and I went to the doctor's appointment know-ing that surgery was in my near future, but that was all we knew. Dr. Coselli looked at my reports and informed us that while the biopsies had confirmed DCIS in one area of my right breast as well as pre-cancer in another area of the same breast, the MRI showed more suspicious areas in both breasts that should be biopsied. It was evident to me at that point that these calcifications-turning-to-can-cer were prevalent in both breasts. I made up my mind at that moment, with Chuck's full support, that I would skip more biopsies and move forward with bilateral mastec-tomies and hopefully be done with breast cancer forever. I did not want a repeat of this experience. And I wanted my surgery done before Christmas.

As we talked through these options with the doc-tor, we realized that I would need a plastic surgeon for reconstruction. Dr. Coselli tried to gently tell me that a surgery before Christmas was unlikely since he and the plastic surgeon would need to coordinate sched-ules as well as coordinate with the operating room. I would need an appointment with the plastic surgeon to decide on a reconstruction method. Then I would need another appointment with Dr. Coselli to go over the entire procedure. Finally, I would have to complete the standard pre-op tests in advance of the surgery. The entire process would take more than three weeks, possibly more than a month. I had no knowledge of plastic surgeons, and Dr. Coselli did not feel he could ethically recommend a specific doctor.

While still sitting in Dr. Coselli's office, I quickly got on the phone with John Barksdale.

"John, what is the name of that plastic surgeon who recommended Dr. Coselli to you?"

Hearing the name of the plastic surgeon, Dr. Coselli said, "Oh, I know him. He's in this building just one floor up. Let me have my receptionist call and set up an appointment." In one phone call, the receptionist found out that the plastic surgeon had an appointment opening that very afternoon. She also found out that both surgeons had a surgery opening on December 13, just 10 days away. All they had to do was find an available operating room. I was told to go ahead and get my pre-op done while I waited for the appointment with the plastic surgeon. Following the plastic surgeon's appointment, I was to come back to Dr. Coselli's office for the final appointment before surgery—*all in one day.*

Later that same afternoon, sitting again in Dr. Coselli's office a little dazed, I looked across the desk at him. He looked at me with a critical eye, "Are you okay? Are you processing this? In one day, you have done what it takes most patients several weeks to do. Are you comfortable with all your decisions today?"

"Yes, yes, I am. I think we knew when we came in here today that this would be my decision. I want this over with."

Two days later, on Wednesday evening, I walked into the worship center to prepare for the service, and I was approached by Lee Maxcy, the Business Administrator, or CFO, of the entire Second Baptist domain. He put his arm around me and said, "Karen, I am so sorry to hear about your diagnosis, but Dr. Young wants me to tell you that Second Baptist will cover all your expenses that insurance does not cover." I was stunned. Tears were beginning to be a regular thing.

Our older daughter, Bonnie, who lives in the Dallas area, came to stay with us for a few days during and after my surgery. Second Baptist Church of Houston not only covered all my expenses but they also paid for my younger daughter, Kelley, to fly from North Carolina to be with us.

Love. I was loved.

One of the precious ladies of our church, June Richards, asked me before surgery how she could help. I knew I would be working right up to the day of my surgery, and I realized there would be no time to decorate for Christmas. And we had moved into a new house just three months before. I would have to rework all my decorations for the new house. June is a premier decorator, and her own home is like something from *Southern Living* magazine, so I did not hesitate.

"Yes!" I cried. "Could you possibly decorate my house for Christmas? I love Christmas, and I just won't have time. I can give you the decorations I have already, and here is my budget for new things."

She was so overjoyed that you would think I had given *her* a gift. Not only did she rework and decorate with what I had, but with her own money, she bought a new tree, decorations, Christmas dishes, chargers, napkins—the works. Our home never felt so festive. Even now, every Christmas when I pull out my Christmas dishes, I remember June and her generous gift of love.

Did I mention that I love Christmas? On December 12, the night before my surgery, Chuck and I were driving into town to stay at the hotel adjacent to the hospital because my report time was 5:00 a.m. As we drove down Post Oak Boulevard, I was overwhelmed by the little white Christmas lights blanketing the trees lining the street. Tears ran down my cheeks as I took in the wondrous sight. "What's wrong? Are you okay?" Chuck was intensely alert to my feelings.

"I just love the Christmas lights."

We decided to get dinner right there on Post Oak at Willie G's, one of my favorite restaurants. While we were dining on fried shrimp and seared sea scallops, I kept craning my neck to look out the window.

"What are you looking at?" Chuck asked.

"I see more Christmas lights over there in that plaza. Can we check them out after dinner?"

"Of course. You don't even have to ask." It was a typical Chuck response.

We drove over to the little plaza and parked the car. As we got out, we were surrounded by a wonderland of Christmas lights on every tree and a magnificent display of huge lighted gifts in the center. We walked around the plaza, holding hands and talking of the upcoming surgery in wonder of God's goodness in working out each detail. We talked of the future and gave thanks for God's many blessings. We drove to the hotel, rested well but briefly, and arose at 4:30 a.m.

Surgery and recovery were painful, extremely painful. But I have never felt so loved. What a blessing it was to have my husband and both my daughters surrounding me. When I think of my cancer days of 2007, I rarely think of the pain. I remember God's blessings that were poured out on me through the love of my family, his people, and his church. Blessings like these are truly joy in the midst of struggle.

Every December 12th, the night before my surgery anniversary, Chuck and I return to Post Oak. We go to dinner at Willie G's and then drive over to Post Oak Plaza. Sometimes it is cold and windy. Sometimes it is warm, and sometimes it is raining. Whatever the weather, we walk hand in hand and look at the lights, remembering the past, looking toward the future, and counting our many blessings.

Are you in the middle of a battle with cancer or some other disease? Do you endure chronic or even acute pain on a daily basis? Are you fighting for your life? In the midst of your crisis, God wants to bless you. He wants to demonstrate his love and care for you. Look for him. Look for him in the doctors and nurses who care for you. Look for him in the attentiveness of your family. Look for him in the expressions of love and care from your friends and church family. He has not abandoned you. When you see him in the tender eyes of your spouse or in the generous gesture from a friend, it is there that you will experience joy.

Sometimes, it is easy to think that you are alone in the pain and suffering. We easily fall into the delusion that we are being punished by God. Do not believe that lie from Satan. The illnesses and ailments in this world are not God's punishment on us but rather the consequences of a fallen world. No one is exempt from the ills and evils that surround us. Some of us want to ask "Why?" when illness befalls us or a loved one. I do not believe there is any answer other than this—life happens. Sin entered the world, unleashing pain, suffering, and destruction. The joy is that we never face the challenge alone.

After your immediate family, your church family is one of the first places to turn for support when you or a loved one is in a physical battle for health. God's Word instructs us to pray for healing and to call the elders to be anointed with oil.

> *Is anyone among you sick? Let him call for the elders of the church, and let them pray over him, anointing him with oil in the name of the Lord.*
> *And the prayer of faith will save the one who is sick, and the Lord will raise him up. And if he has committed sins, he will be forgiven.*
> —James 5:14–15

Our current church, West University Baptist, has a healing service each Wednesday evening where those with physical or spiritual ailments can come and share their needs. Those in our faithful group of prayer warriors gather around, lay on hands, and supplicate our Great Physician for his healing power while one of our pastors anoints the individual with oil. We know God has the power to heal. Jesus healed countless infirmities of the lame, the blind, and the ill.[5] We also know that not everyone is healed here on earth. Our journey with Fred is a testament to that, yet God is still faithful. We so often forget that our healing will be truly complete on that day we are united with our Savior face to face. In heaven, there is no sickness, blindness, or pain—only fullness of joy.

Do you know someone who is going through cancer treatment or some other physical trial? Be a blessing to them. Allow God to use you to demonstrate his love and be a vessel of his joy in their struggle. Bake those cookies. Write that card. Make that visit. Pray for their healing. Be the carrier of God's joy to someone in need today.

Chapter 11

Victim or Victor?

There are so many things in this world over which we have no control. Life's circumstances can quickly defeat us. At some time in our lives, we all face those tragedies or situations that take us into a dark, defeated place. Why is it so hard to get back up and stand once we have been brought low by life? What should we do when we find ourselves victims in that shadowy dungeon of defeat? How do we break free and climb out of the pit?

Several years ago, I found myself a victim, living in that dungeon of defeat. I had recently undergone my bilateral mastectomies due to cancer in both breasts.

The surgery and resulting reconstruction left me feeling rather artificial and disfigured. Shortly after that trauma, I gave up my dream job of a lifetime to follow God's calling for my husband to be part of a new church plant.

The decision to leave Second Baptist Church, the "big church," was not one we took lightly or made quickly. It was a great church with amazing ministries and dear friends. The issue for us was Chuck's calling and ministry. His passion in ministry had always been for international missions. We had served with the International Mission Board for more than six years, and then he served as a missions pastor for 10 years. He was all about God's people engaging the world with the message of Jesus Christ.

There were changes at our church when it merged with Second Baptist Church, and Chuck's responsibilities changed as well. The larger church already had a missions pastor, so Chuck was placed in a different role within the sizable church staff. He gave all he had to his new responsibilities but lacked the passion to sustain his efforts. After four years, he began to feel that he was punching a time clock for God just to get a paycheck. It didn't feel right. His desire was to get back to missions, his calling. At the same time, our campus pastor, Doug Page, was considering beginning a new church with a strong emphasis on international missions. He invited Chuck to help with the church startup and lead as the missions pastor. We spent many hours in prayer seeking God's will. It was a difficult offer to turn down.

Although Chuck had been displaced over the four years, I had, in fact, found my sweet spot in ministry. I had a passion for worship and all the moving parts that went into planning and executing a worship service. I also enjoyed assisting with the seasonal events such as the Christmas or Easter programs or pageants. My participation had always been on a volunteer basis until the merger. Second Baptist hired me to do those things I loved. I worked alongside the best worship pastor I had ever known, Mark Terry, who was also a dear friend. I was thriving.

When I took the job of worship and special events coordinator, I promised Chuck that his calling and his ministry came first. If there was ever a time that God would call him to a different place, I assured him that I would be right there at his side. As we began to pray about this new church startup possibility, I knew that time had come. It was time for Chuck to get back to the ministry and passion that God had given him.

Leaving a large church can be complicated, so we continued to pray and plan. Finally, the day came to make our decision public. Within 30 minutes of handing in our letters of resignation, our church phones and computers were taken. We were asked to pack up and leave the premises. It was a hard day. There were no sweet farewells, receptions, or love offerings.

While the actions of the church may seem harsh, I must in hindsight defend them. Just as any large corporation must protect itself, a mega church has the same issues. Sadly, access to databases, financials, and membership records must be protected from those who would do the church harm. Although I was not one of those, the policy rightfully had to be carried out.

In spite of understanding the policy, I was traumatized. I was left with no phone, no computer, and thus no access to our own personal bank account. I found myself crying at a Kinko's computer desk trying to get into our account without a phone to receive the authentication code. All my contacts were gone. I couldn't even call Chuck because his phone was gone, too. Before leaving the church, I had quickly thought to call Doug, the new pastor of our yet-to-be-founded church. He told me to go to the Verizon store and set up an account for our church plant and get phones for each of us. At least I had a car. Within a few days, with new phones and new computers, we began to build our new existence.

The decision to leave our church family came with many changes. Some we expected and understood, and others were totally unexpected. While our decision impacted us in some obvious ways, it also impacted those we left behind. Some were shocked, some sad, and others angry and confused. We did not have the opportunity to say goodbye and explain all that God had shown us and what he had called us to do. Many of our friends' questions were left unanswered, leaving them feeling abandoned. Some of our dearest friends were suffering great losses of their own. In particular, Mark, my boss and worship pastor, and his wife, Sonya, had been good friends with all of us who left to begin the new church. They had been especially good friends to me. We all had been a close-knit group, but Mark and Sonya were left behind. God had not called them to this new work with us. He had given them a special calling to remain. In addition to our group leaving the church, Mark also lost his worship associate and good friend who had been called as worship pastor at a large church in East Texas. Mark and Sonya's losses were great.

As soon as I had my new phone set up, I added Mark's and Sonya's numbers and texted them with my new number. I received no response. A while later, I tried to call to check in with my dearest friends. The calls went to voicemail. Over the next several weeks, after many attempts to reach them, I finally received a text from Mark. I don't recall the exact words, but it basically said they did not want to communicate with us. They were hurting, and while they still loved Chuck and me and considered us family, things would never be the same. I know now that Mark and Sonya were acting out of their own pain and attempting to protect themselves from further injury. However, I was devastated and confused. I had just lost my dream job and the best friends I had ever had.

I was in a trifecta of loss—breasts, job, and friends. Without realizing it, I was a victim of circumstance and depression. I couldn't focus. I couldn't concentrate. I was sad. Doug, my new boss and pastor, was confused. What had happened to the efficient and effective worker he had known before? Why weren't things getting done? I was floundering. After many weeks of seeing me struggle, Doug wisely suggested a counselor to help me process all I had been through.

In our first encounter, the therapist helped me understand I was grieving—grieving for the loss of my job I had loved, grieving for friendships lost, and grieving for my breasts. She showed me a list of the stages of grief: denial, anger, bargaining, depression, and acceptance.

"What stage would you say you are in currently?" she asked.

"I think I'm doing them all at the same time," I wailed.

"I do, too," the counselor compassionately affirmed.

In short, I was a mess. The biggest thing the therapist did for me that first day was validate my feelings. They were justified. In the sessions that followed, I was able to process my grief and move forward. I regained my focus and found my stride. I was climbing out of the dark dungeon of defeat and depression. There was just one problem.

I ate. I overate. My once disciplined self was out of control. Without realizing what I was doing, I was sabotaging myself. I seemed to love food more than I loved myself. Only recently have I realized what was happening to me. In all my recovery from loss, and even after the restoration of cherished friendships, I continued to view myself as a victim. I was a victim of cancer. I was a victim of rejection. I was a victim of life. Even though I was no longer in a state of grief, I was still living as a victim. In my own eyes, I was damaged goods.

I had forgotten one vital truth. Jesus conquered sin, death, and suffering by dying on the cross and through his resurrection. Jesus not only lifts us out of our pit of grief and depression, but he has defeated every force and every thought that would victimize us. His love has conquered all. We are victors!

Who shall separate us from the love of Christ? Shall tribulation, or distress, or persecution, or famine, or nakedness, or danger, or sword? . . . No, in all these things we are more than conquerors through him who loved us. *For I am sure that neither death nor life, nor angels nor rulers, nor things present nor things to come, nor powers, nor height nor depth, nor anything else in all creation, will be able to separate us from the love of God in Christ Jesus our Lord* (emphasis added).

—Rom. 8:35, 37–39

Grief and depression often go hand in hand. Our losses can leave us down and depressed, not allowing us to move to that final stage of grief—acceptance. At some point, we must come to the realization that life has changed. It will never again be as it was. I had to accept that my body would never be as it was. I had to accept that I would no longer sit in Mark's office with the worship staff planning a Christmas extravaganza. I would never again walk into that empty worship center early on Sunday morning to find only Mark there with my venti decaf extra shot soy latte waiting for me. I had to accept that there would be no more lunches and heart-to-heart talks with Sonya.

Acceptance seems cruel and painful, but it is what allows us to move forward instead of always looking back. Acceptance comes with claiming victory. Allow God to lift your chin, dear friend, and see what he has ahead of you.

O Lord, how many are my foes!
*   Many are rising against me;*
many are saying of my soul,
*   "There is no salvation for him in God."*

But you, O Lord, are a shield about me,
*   my glory, and the lifter of my head.*
I cried aloud to the Lord,
*   and he answered me from his holy hill. Selah*

I lay down and slept;
*   I woke again, for the Lord sustained me.*
I will not be afraid of many thousands of people
*   who have set themselves against me all around.*

Arise, O Lord!
*   Save me, O my God!*
For you strike all my enemies on the cheek;
*   you break the teeth of the wicked.*

Salvation belongs to the LORD;
your blessing be on your people! Selah

—Ps. 3:1-8

At some time or another in our lives, almost all of us experience a season of despair, a period of desperation when nothing seems to be going right. The stress and anxiety mount, and prayer seems like little more than wishing on a penny tossed into a fountain. Faith can be hard to come by in the midst of depression, despair, and desperation, yet I have found that these are the times that God comes to me in very real and tangible ways, demonstrating his love for me.

In Psalm 3, David's desperation is palpable. He feels attacked from all sides, yet he says that God is the lifter of his head. The picture this evokes in my little brain is of a bullied little girl who has just endured a bitter day at school. The mean girls have teased her about her dress, her hair, the way she eats, and what she eats. She is too skinny and wears homemade dresses. Instead of peanut butter and jelly sandwiches, she eats tuna on crackers. She is not acceptable. She is different. They have ruthlessly teased her and made her the laughing stock of the classroom. As she walks home from school, her eyes don't leave the sidewalk while the tears drip just ahead of her shoes. When she arrives home, her daddy providentially meets her on the porch.

"What's wrong, Precious? Did you have a bad day at school?"

Not able to look up, she just nods as more tears fall, this time making their mark on her sneakers. Then her knowing and wise father reaches down and with his fingers gently lifts her chin upward so she can see the love and acceptance in his eyes. The pain melts away in the loving, accepting gaze of her father.

We may not have an army encamped around us ready to attack as David did, but our enemies are real—rejection, loss, illness, pain, and so many other crises. Just like David and just like our bullied little girl, our Heavenly Father is reaching down to us, gently lifting our heads so we might meet his eyes and feel his love and comfort. Look up, child. Look up into your Father's eyes. He wants you to rely on him, to trust him. God's Word is full of promises of his faithfulness and care for his children. He loves you unconditionally and will care for you. He will see you through your crisis and bring you out of your despair. Let him lift your head. Have you allowed your life's circumstances and struggles to oppress, depress, and defeat you? Turn to Jesus. His love has already won the war. Claim victory, my friend.

Often, one of the big crises of our lives is an economical one. I don't believe we can make deals with God, but we most certainly can trust his promises. If we are generous, he will be generous with us. It's a promise. Look at what God did for a widow and her son when he sent Elijah for a visit in her time of desperation.

Then the word of the LORD came to him [Elijah], "Arise, go to Zarephath, which belongs to Sidon, and dwell there. Behold, I have commanded a widow there to feed you." So he arose and went to Zarephath. And when he came to the gate of the city, behold, a widow was there gathering sticks. And he called to her and said, "Bring me a little water in a vessel, that I may drink." And as she was going to bring it, he called to her and said, "Bring me a morsel of bread in your hand." And she said, "As the LORD your God lives, I have nothing baked, only a handful of flour in a jar and a little oil in a jug. And now I am gathering a couple of sticks that I may go in and prepare it for myself and my son, that we may eat it and die." And Elijah said to her, "Do not fear; go and do as you have said. But first make me a little cake of it and bring it to me, and afterward make something for yourself and your son. For thus says the LORD, the God of Israel,

'The jar of flour shall not be spent, and the jug of oil shall not be empty, until the day that the LORD sends rain upon the earth.'" And she went and did as Elijah said. And she and he and her household ate for many days. The jar of flour was not spent, neither did the jug of oil become empty, according to the word of the LORD that he spoke by Elijah.

—1 Kings 17:8–16

Imagine the relief and comfort this woman experienced as God met her physical need. Our God, the creator of the universe, not only made something out of nothing when he created time and space, but he also creates much out of little. God makes himself known and demonstrates his love and his greatness as he fulfills his role of Provider.

There was another poor widow in the Old Testament. In her desperation, she reached out to the prophet Elisha for help. She was down to nothing but a little oil in her pantry.

Now the wife of one of the sons of the prophets cried to Elisha, "Your servant my husband is dead, and you know that your servant feared the LORD, but the creditor has come to take my two children to be his slaves." And Elisha said to her, "What shall I do for you? Tell me; what have you in the house?" And she said, "Your servant has nothing in the house except a jar of oil." Then he said, "Go outside, borrow vessels from all your neighbors, empty vessels and not too few. Then go in and shut the door behind yourself and your sons and pour into all these vessels. And when one is full, set it aside." So she went from him and shut the door behind herself and her sons. And as she poured they brought the vessels to her. When the vessels were full, she said to her son, "Bring me another vessel." And he said to her, "There is not another." Then the oil stopped flowing. She came and told the man of God, and he said, "Go, sell the oil and pay your debts, and you and your sons can live on the rest."

—2 Kings 4:1–7

The creditors were calling this poor widow at all hours. They were going to take her sons as slaves to pay off her obligation. Have you ever lived that nightmare? You don't answer the phone because the relentless bill collectors have your number. Every call is another credit card company. You dread opening the mail only to find more bills with a big red past due stamp or more notices from relentless collection agencies. It's an anxiety like no other. You say to yourself, "What should I do? Do I need to get a second or third job? Where can I find more money? This nausea won't go away. Which bills do I pay, and which ones can wait?"

Chuck and I have lived that nightmare. We came back from the mission field with a significant amount of debt. On top of that debt came expenses first for one daughter in college and then the second. We were trying to help them out as much as possible to keep their student loans to a minimum. We had made a few bad decisions, and before we knew it, we were behind on everything. The only things not overdue were the utilities. We had credit card debt, department store debt, personal loan debt, car debt, as well as a house note to pay. All of them were behind. I had stopped answering the phone and just let "the machine" get it. Sometimes, I didn't even listen to the messages. It was too depressing. Chuck and I were both working full-time and trying to make good decisions, but the hole was too deep. We finally realized there was no way out. We had to sell our house; otherwise, we would be in foreclosure within a few weeks.

We put our house on the market and prayed for a buyer. Quickly please, Lord! The buyer never came, but the foreclosure notice did. In the meantime, Richard, one of the deacons in our church, noticed the For Sale sign in front of our house. He approached me at church the next Sunday.

"So I noticed your house is for sale. Are you planning on moving away? What's going on?" he inquired.

"No, we just need to downsize. We're trying to cut expenses a bit." Something in my voice or perhaps just the Holy Spirit tipped him off.

"Are you two having financial issues?"

"Well," my voice cracked, "we are kind of behind."

Richard was a financial planner, so he proposed meeting with Chuck and me to go over our financials and see if he could come up with a plan to get us out of debt. I told Chuck about Richard's offer, and we promptly set up an appointment. We were hopeful.

Richard poured over our statements and past due notices. He read the fine print on the foreclosure notice. He added, crunched numbers, and sighed.

"I don't see any way out of this except bankruptcy. You are just too far behind."

My previously hopeful heart sank.

Chuck was somewhat stoic. "If I can't pay back everything I owe, then I'll have to leave the ministry," was

Chuck's response. "I can't be a minister of the gospel if I have defaulted on my own obligations. I would feel like a fraud. I'll just have to find a secular job."

"Now wait, you don't have to be so rash," Richard responded. "Bankruptcy is totally legal and created for situations just like this. There is no shame in using the resources available to you."

"I understand that it's a legal option, but this is my personal conviction before God that a minister should pay his debts. I just wouldn't feel right about it. If there is no other way, I'll go talk to the pastor and resign right away."

Richard began crunching numbers again. Chuck and I were silent as we contemplated a future outside full-time ministry. What did that look like? What kind of job could Chuck apply for? Where would we live? Could our girls finish college?

Richard interrupted our morose thoughts. "I have another proposal for you. I will set you up on a budget and lend you the money to pay off your debts and get your house out of foreclosure. You will then only have to pay your house note, utilities, and a payment to me every month until the debt is paid off."

We were stunned. Even with our own financial mistakes and mismanagement, God was still proving himself faithful as our Provider. We were going to be able to keep our home and would have an interest-free consolidation loan. There would be no more bill collectors calling. There would be no more stress over which bills to pay. Chuck would not have to resign. The relief and gratitude brought us both to tears. We were no longer victims of our own making. God had just reached out to us in love and lifted our heads.

Richard followed through with a payment to each of our creditors. He also personally went to the auction to buy our house out of foreclosure right before it was to be taken from us. It took us several years to pay off our debt to Richard, but we will forever be gratefully indebted to him and to God for his provision. Sometimes, God lifts our head with a gaze of love, sometimes with never-ending oil, and sometimes through a godly man named Richard.

Whether you're a victim of loss, rejection, or financial crisis, God is on your side. Do not let grief, despair, or depression keep your eyes downcast. Jesus has fought the enemy and won the battle. His resurrected life is proof of his power over every force that would bring you low. Lift your head, friend. Look up to the one who is your comfort, your refuge, your strength, and your provider. In him, you can claim victory.

Chapter 12

Remember

That which was from the beginning, which we have heard, which we have seen with our eyes, which we looked upon and have touched with our hands, concerning the word of life—the life was made manifest, and we have seen it, and testify to it and proclaim to you the eternal life, which was with the Father and was made manifest to us—that which we have seen and heard we proclaim also to you, so that you too may have fellowship with us; and indeed our

fellowship is with the Father and with his Son Jesus Christ. And we are writing these things so that our joy may be complete.

—1 John 1:1–4

One day as I was having my alone time with God, I reflected on the many trials of my life and on God's faithfulness in each instance, in each valley, on every ugly day. He has been my Rock, my Fortress, the one who held me close when the pain was so great I couldn't even pray. He was my Warm Place in the Sun who brought comfort to my soul in the darkness. It was through this reflection and remembering that God compelled me to write this book.

Just as John wrote of the disciples' compulsion to share all they had seen and heard during their precious time with Jesus, it is through sharing God's faithfulness with you that my joy has been made complete. It is my desire and my purpose that you, too, may experience the faithful strength, love, and comfort of God in your time of need. Part of the joy that comes through trial is knowing that God will use our experiences to encourage and strengthen others.

Remembering also fortifies us for the next round of battle. Each trial has prepared me for the next. As I have experienced God's faithfulness in the small things such as school clothes and Easter dresses, my faith has grown bigger to prepare me for the larger challenges. Easter dresses led to tires and tires to culture shock recovery in Costa Rica. Costa Rica led to confronting opposition and challenges in Spain. Spain led to the later trials of church division and even depression and rejection. While each previous trial in no way removed the pain from the future circumstances, each trial proved the faithfulness of my God. He is big enough, strong enough, and loves me enough to see me through *anything*—even my greatest thorn or fears.

Whatever you are going through now, friend, look back. What has God done for you in the past? How has he provided for you? How has he sustained and encouraged you? Remember those times he has walked with you and given you peace. Remembering is a tool David used often in the Psalms. When he was discouraged, he wrote down the many things God had done for Israel as well as for him personally.

> *Oh give thanks to the Lord; call upon his name;*
> *make known his deeds among the peoples!*
> *Sing to him, sing praises to him;*
> *tell of all his wondrous works!*

Glory in his holy name;
    let the hearts of those who seek the LORD rejoice!
Seek the LORD and his strength;
    seek his presence continually!
Remember the wondrous works that he has done,
    his miracles, and the judgments he uttered,
O offspring of Abraham, his servant,
    children of Jacob, his chosen ones!
                              —Ps. 105:1–6

In the rest of Psalm 105, David goes on to recount God's faithfulness throughout Israel's existence, from the first covenant with Abraham through captivity and then to deliverance from Egypt and every trial and provision in the wilderness. David ends the psalm like this:

So he brought his people out with joy,
    his chosen ones with singing.
And he gave them the lands of the nations,
    and they took possession of the fruit of the peoples' toil,
that they might keep his statutes
    and observe his laws.
Praise the LORD!
                              —Ps. 105:43–45

David's writings reminded Israel—and they remind us today—to look back, to remember the faithfulness of God. He reminds us to recall God's great deeds both in scripture and in our own lives. Here is another personal testimony from David:

> *I waited patiently for the LORD;*
> *he inclined to me and heard my cry.*
> *He drew me up from the pit of destruction,*
> *out of the miry bog,*
> *and set my feet upon a rock,*
> *making my steps secure.*
> *He put a new song in my mouth,*
> *a song of praise to our God.*
> *Many will see and fear,*
> *and put their trust in the LORD.*
> —Ps. 40:1–3

Reading scripture, especially the Psalms, reminds us of the greatness of our God. When I read the Psalms, when I know the suffering David endured in his lifetime, including his huge mistakes, I am inspired by his faith and by his praise. I am encouraged by his honest despair that turns to joy. I am cheered when I see God meet the physical needs of a widow in the Old Testament. I am reassured when I read about God's gentle care for a prophet in depression in the wilderness. During my darkest days in Spain, it was God's Word and its revelation of who God is that sustained me.

After about a year in Mallorca and well after my encounter and reconciliation with Conchita, she came to me with a request. Conchita's mother, Doña Amparo, was a precious, elderly member of our little church. As a result of diabetes, Doña Amparo was totally blind. This slender, tall, yet hunched over 80-year-old with her cane in hand was always ready with the typical Spanish double kisses for me whenever she heard my voice. She and her husband lived with Conchita's family where they could receive the continual care and attention they needed. While Doña Amparo had the complete audible Bible on tape, she was lacking in Bible study material. Knowing it was a big request, Conchita came to me humbly one day to inquire if I could possibly begin recording Bible study materials for her mother. There was no way I could refuse. This was an opportunity to do something for a precious elderly lady who loved the Lord. Even in her advanced years, she was longing to go deeper with God.

I bought a little cassette recorder (this was back in 1991—no flash drives or MP3 players yet). With an already full schedule of home schooling the girls, youth activities, and Bible studies to prepare for teaching, not to mention meal prep and housework, my only time to record these studies for Doña Amparo was at 4:00 in the morning. For our entire last year in Mallorca, every morning I got up, grabbed a cup of coffee, and sat at the computer. I did my own personal Bible study and devotional time and typed my reflections in my computer journal in English. Then I turned on the recorder and read the scripture to Doña Amparo, in Spanish, of course. Then, while reading my journal written in English, I verbally translated my notes for Doña Amparo. Each week, we exchanged tapes. She listened to my tape from the previous week while I recorded a new one.

You might think these 4:00 a.m. recording sessions were a burden, but they were, in fact, my lifeline. My ministry to Doña Amparo was God's gift to me. They kept me in the Word so God could minister to my aching soul. Some weeks were harder than others, and at times my reflections were a little shallow. Doña Amparo would sweetly let me know if I was slacking. "The study was a little light this week," she sweetly commented sometimes when we exchanged tapes and kisses on Sunday. Gratefully, with her discerning spirit, she was aware of all the turmoil and stress the little church body was creating in our lives at that time. She usually recorded a thoughtful message at the end of the tape to encourage me. It was a precious gesture on her part, but in reality, it was studying God's Word that enabled me to survive. He helped me remember who he is and all that he has done and will do for his children.

The Word of God is that sword for our battle. I find it interesting that all the rest of the armor of God is defensive—a helmet, a belt, a shield—to protect us from Satan's darts. The sword is our only offensive weapon. Defense only works for a while. Any good soldier will tell you that. Eventually, we must fight back against Satan's attacks. At some point, we need to go on the offense. What did Jesus use when Satan attacked him in the wilderness? What was his weapon? Scripture!

It is written, "Man shall not live by bread alone."
—Matt. 4:4

Again, it is written, "You shall not put the Lord your God to the test."
—Matt. 4:7

Be gone, Satan! For it is written, "You shall worship the Lord your God and him only shall you serve."
—Matt. 4:10

The battle rages in the spiritual realm whether we are aware of it or not. The only way to arm ourselves is with the Word of God. Read it. Meditate on it. Memorize those verses that reinforce your faith. Use a combination of scriptures and your personal memories of God's faithfulness to make you strong and ready for battle. The trials will come, but the God of the past is also the God of the future and the God of our now.

Jesus Christ is the same yesterday and today and forever.

—Heb. 13:8

There is an important final step in remembering— sharing. As David reflected on the God of Israel's past, he wanted to be sure the generations to come would know of God's great deeds and faithfulness to Israel. He urged his people to share this great history with their children and grandchildren.

He established a testimony in Jacob
*   and appointed a law in Israel,*
which he commanded our fathers
*   to teach to their children,*
that the next generation might know them,
*   the children yet unborn,*

and arise and tell them to their children,
so that they should set their hope in God
and not forget the works of God,
but keep his commandments.

—Ps. 78:5–7

Here is a challenge for you. Do your children or other loved ones in your life know what God has done for you? First of all, do they know that he redeemed you with the blood of Jesus? Do they know that you have trusted him with your life and your eternity? Have you told them how God has been faithful in your life to provide for you or to give you strength when you were weak? Do they know how he lifted you up when you couldn't go on, how he carried you?

Recount each story time and again. Our survival stories are their legacy. Be like the old gray-haired soldier who tells how his fellow soldier rescued him as he lay wounded on the battlefield. He tells that same story over and over again to his grandchildren gathered at his feet—a story of heroism and victory. The hero in your story is Jesus, and the victory is his. You are not bragging when you share your victories. You are sharing the wonders of your God.

In each memory I have shared, in each battle I have faced, I know I am merely a weak soldier who God has rescued. Each time, he picked me up from the battle-field, put a sword in my hand, and whispered in my ear, "I've got you, child. Hold up your sword and fight. I have already won this battle." As God reminded Israel, he is the one who has sustained us, provided for us, and liberated us.

> *And when the Lord your God brings you into the land that he swore to your fathers, to Abraham, to Isaac, and to Jacob, to give you—with great and good cities that you did not build, and houses full of all good things that you did not fill, and cisterns that you did not dig, and vineyards and olive trees that you did not plant—and when you eat and are full, then take care lest you forget the Lord, who brought you out of the land of Egypt, out of the house of slavery. It is the Lord your God you shall fear. Him you shall serve and by his name you shall swear.*
>
> —Deut. 6:10–13

You may not be in a place of remembering today. You may be crying out, "How do I get through this?" Whether you are grieving the loss of a loved one or a child, or whether you are experiencing unbearable loneliness, God has not forgotten you. Divorce, rejection, or illness may have laid you out flat. You may be lying on the battlefield right now awaiting rescue. You may be searching in the darkness for God's light and warmth. Trust him, friend. Pick up your Bible and begin in the Psalms. If you can't feel his strength, be comforted by the truth of who he is and what he has done in the past. His faithfulness dictates that he will care for you, too.

Another tool that has served me well in remembering is a prayer journal. I have stacks and stacks of old prayer journals dating back to our first years of ministry while Chuck was still in school. I received my first prayer journal at a women's retreat. Our pastor's wife had created personalized, lace-trimmed, padded notebooks for each woman at the retreat. Padded photo albums and padded picture frames were big in the late 1970s. I had those frilly picture frames all over my house. I remember the retreat well because I left Chuck at home with our two daughters who were sick with the chicken pox. I also left instructions to soothe them with soda baths and calamine lotion. At the retreat, while I was trying not to worry about my sick girls and their daddy, our pastor's wife shared the importance of documenting our faith walk. I began right then to document my worry, and when I arrived home, I received my first answered prayer to record. Chuck and the girls had not only survived the soda baths and calamine lotion, but they had also enjoyed a special bonding time.

Since that time, I have made a habit of writing my prayers to God along with any verses that have spoken to me that day as I read the Word. I write down my struggles as well as God's victories. I sometimes hurriedly scratch down a concern and then feel I am rushing my time with God. But even when I am rushed, there is a sense of release. I am turning my requests over to God rather than rushing out the door bearing the load alone. The simple task of writing down the struggles and the joys reinforces in me the confidence I have in my Lord that he is reading over my shoulder and pressing into me. I encourage you to try prayer journaling. I believe you will be blessed.

I want to share one last scripture with you. It is one of those passages that has inspired and encouraged me throughout these many years of ministry. It is my prayer for you.

For this reason I bow my knees before the Father, from whom every family in heaven and on earth is named, that according to the riches of his glory he may grant you to be strengthened with power through his Spirit in your inner being, so that Christ may dwell in your hearts through faith—that you, being rooted and grounded in love, may have strength to comprehend with all the saints what is the breadth and length and height and depth, and to know the love of Christ that surpasses knowledge, that you may be filled with all the fullness of God.

Now to him who is able to do far more abundantly than all that we ask or think, according to the power at work within us, to him be glory in the church and in Christ Jesus throughout all generations, forever and ever. Amen.

—Eph. 3:14–21

God is able, friend, to do more than you think you need. He is able to do more than you can ask. He is able to do more than you can imagine. Allow God's power to work in you. As a result, you will find joy, and he will be glorified now and in the generations to come. Allow him today to fill you with joy in your struggle. Even in your darkness, he truly is your Warm Place in the Sun.

Notes

Chapter 4: Why, God?

1. 1 Sam. 16–18.

2. 1 Sam. 18–27.

3. 2 Sam. 15–17.

Chapter 6: Just Keep Showing Up

1. Charles Dickens, *A Tale of Two Cities*, Project Gutenberg. https://www. gutenberg.org/files/98/98-h/98-h.htm.

2. Jim Gilbert, "I Love You with the Love of the Lord," copyright © 1977 Bud John Songs (ASCAP) (adm. at CapitolCMGPublishing.com), all rights reserved, used by permission.

Chapter 7: Lessons from Bloody Knees

1. 1 Sam. 17:34–37.

2. Acts 7:30.

3. John 10:3–15.

4. Acts 9, 13, 14.

5. Acts 9:23, 14:19, 16:19–24, 21:30–28:31; Col. 1:24–29; 2 Tim. 3:11.

Chapter 8: But It's My Fault

1. 1 Sam. 9–13.

2. 1 Sam. 15.

3. 2 Sam. 11.

4. Matt. 8:24, 14:13, 14:23, 15:21, 21:17; Mark 1:35, 3:7, 4:35–38, 6:31–32, 6:45–46, 7:24; Luke 5:16, 6:12, 8:22–23, 9:10, 9:28, 22:39; John 6:15, 8:1.

5. 2 Sam. 11:2–4.

6. 2 Sam. 11:5–27.

7. 2 Sam. 12:15–19.

8. 2 Sam. 13–16.

9. Luke 15:22–24.

Chapter 9: But It Hurts! When God's People Are Ungodly

1. Acts 9:23–24, 9:29, 14:5–7, 14:19, 16:20–24, 17:13, 18:6; Acts 21–28.

2. 1 Sam. 16:11, 17:34–37.

3. Isa. 35:4, 41:10; Matt. 1:20, 28:10; Luke 1:30, 2:10.

Chapter 10: That's Life

1. Job 1:13–19.

2. Job 2–37.

3. Gen. 3:14–19.

4. Rom. 3:23.

5. Matt. 8:5–13; 9:1–8, 18–33; 12:10–13; 15:22–28; 20:30–34. Mark 1:30–31, 40–45; 7:31–37; 8:22–26. Luke 7:11–18, 8:43–48, 13:10–17, 14:1–4, 17:11–19, 22:50–51. John 4:46–47, 5:1–9, 9:1–38, 11:1–46.